HEARTSPEAK: ☪
TIME FOR TRUTH
An Archangel's Answer Guide for Humanity

HEARTSPEAK: ☾
TIME FOR TRUTH
An Archangel's Answer Guide for Humanity

KATHI CASTELLUCCIO

WINGMARK PRESS

Copyright © 2018 by Kathleen Castelluccio

Published by Wingmark Press
P.O. Box 83, West Chicago, IL 60186

Copy Editor: Janet Williams
Design & Illustration: Kathi Castelluccio

All rights reserved. No part of this publication may be reproduced, distributed or transmitted in any manner without written permission of the copyright owner or publisher, except for the use of quotations within critical reviews and other noncommercial uses permitted by copyright law.

This book is not intended as a substitute for professional medical advice. The reader should consult a physician in matters relating to health and with respect to any symptoms that may require diagnosis or medical attention.

ISBN 978-0-9600121-8-3 (softbound)
ISBN 978-0-9600121-9-0 (paper over board)

Printed in the United States of America

First Edition

Dedication ♡

To my dear mother and friend, Janet Williams, I devote this book. Without her nurturing and support, this embodiment of work would not have been possible. It was through her loving guidance that I was raised without prejudice in a spiritual and progressive home, open to all possibility in a quest for truth and equality. My mother has been my mentor and guide throughout my life and was instrumental in launching my confidence to publish this book. As an educator and a seeker of "all things possible", her vast knowledge of worldly and other-worldly truth helped confirm the information received through my heart. Not only did she serve as a sounding board but also an editor, utilizing her vast knowledge of the English language to help proofread and punctuate the material received from Archangel Gabriel.

On a daily basis, I give thanks to God and Archangel Gabriel for enabling me to receive the messages contained within this book. This material, along with hundreds of additional messages, has changed my perspective and life, as well as helped many others. Out of gratitude and soul-purpose, I published this book to share these insights and truths with the world.

Without the devotion of my family and amazing friends, I would not have had the time, energy or confidence to pursue this endeavor. My husband Joe, through his loving support, has enabled me to work from home to nurture our children and my gifted abilities. He is my soul mate and the most amazingly strong, yet sensitive, person I know, adding stability, warmth and fun to our ever-changing world. Our precious children, Joelle, Nicholas, Jenna and Colette, are clear examples of life's beauty, love and individuality, adding great depth and joy to our lives. For all of the beautiful souls that grace my life with Light, I will forever be grateful!

Contents

Section I: Introduction into Discovery
- My Discovery & Life-Awakening 3
- Visible Evidence: The Rainbow Light 9
- God's Messages 13
- Defining Channeling, Angels & Souls 16
- Archangel Gabriel 19

Section II: Humanity's Misconceptions & Actual Truths
- The Power-of-Being 27
- Truth with a Capital "T" 32
- Energy 38
- The Plight of Mankind 46
- Your Significance in the Interwoven World 52
- Humanity's Damaging Limitations of God 57
- Unconditional Love 62
- Life Lessons 67
- Mind-Created Realities & Justification 72
- The Underlying Factors of Miscommunication 79
- Struggle & Strife 86
- Fear & False-Fear 91
- Worry of the Mind 96
- Guilt & Self-Punishment 102
- Anger & Depression 107
- The Coiled-Up State of Defensiveness 113
- Suppression 117
- Relationships 122
- Homosexuality & Human Prejudice 127
- Children & Growth 130
- Career Path 135
- Health & Well-being 141
- Disasters & Negative Energy 146
- Death of the Body–Ascent of the Soul 154

Section III: Individual Purpose & Self-Discovery

Shine Your Light 165
Life is a Journey! 167
Unearth Your Purpose & Your Path 172
Unravel Your Truth & Spin Your Dream 177
Weave Your Life's Tapestry with Joy 182
Piece Together the Greater Picture 187
Cherish Yourself 193

Section IV: God's Greater Wisdom & Ever-Presence

God's Unfolding Truths 201
God the Almighty 207
The Light of God 213
Universal Energy 218
Nature: God's Glory 223

Section V: Tools for Transformation & Creation

Nature's Healing Essence 231
Prayer 235
Sleep 241
Meditation 244
The Mind's Eye 249
Body Movement & Nourishment 252
Healing 256
Inner Guidance 260
Wisdom of the Heart 264
Living Through the Heart 268
Gratitude 274
Capturing Time 277
Conscious Living 283
The Flow of Life 288
Staying on Course 290

Section I
Introduction into Discovery

In order to be lifted to see all that shines freely in the world,

you must open your eyes, mind and heart.

In order to spread that Light of truth and help others to see,

you must open the lines of communication and

bridge the gap that separates mankind.

My Discovery & Life-Awakening

Something inside of me kept urging and urging me to sit down at my computer and simply type...type for no reason...type without thinking... type to discover some magical thing. I pushed that crazy urge aside, again and again. I was too busy, too logical, too organized, and I had things to do...never-ending things, and never enough time to do them. I couldn't waste valuable time that needed to be devoted elsewhere—to my husband and four kids, to the family finances that were in a shambles, to my freelance design work, to the house cleaning, organizing and unending projects. So I pushed that urge aside, along with anything else that was "not important"...until everything fell apart! Out of desperation, I finally gave in to that crazy urge and what I discovered was a miracle—a miracle that would change my life forever!

Ever since I was a child, everything came easily to me...everything except obtaining joy and self-confidence. I knew my life was blessed, but I felt lost—continually battling feelings of depression. From birth I was extremely sensitive and painfully shy. My heart would literally ache when I witnessed cruelty or another's pain. I could not understand why the world was so unjust and, even as a small child, I longed for a deeper understanding. I lived my life on auto-pilot simply waiting to get to the next stage of life, hoping that once I arrived I would discover joy.

Being a perfectionist, this joy did not appear as I lived life striving to accomplish what I was "supposed to" rather than addressing my own needs. This "just-existing" version of life continued until the summer of 2006 when it came to a screeching halt. My husband lost his business—a business that had already depleted our life-savings and financial resources.

We were in extreme financial debt. My husband was experiencing health problems. Both of us now battled feelings of depression. We had 6-year-old triplets and a 5-year-old to physically, emotionally and spiritually provide for. I had given up my career to raise our children, resulting in earning from home a freelance income that could not support our family. The only assets we had left were our house...and our treasured families.

Our family and friends pulled us through, providing tremendous emotional and financial support at that mind-crippling time. Our reliance upon them instilled gratitude, but it also uncovered feelings of helplessness and a lack of confidence in our own resources—something that we had not experienced before. Being a planner, a thinker and a problem solver, I struggled to find a solution that would provide an answer to everything—finances, employment, health issues and the maintenance of a healthy, nurturing environment for our children. My mind could not find a logical solution and I was worried and stressed. I needed answers and there was nowhere else to turn. That is when I decided to just let go and follow that urge that had been nagging at me for years...

November 10, 2006:
Exactly at midnight I sat down at my computer, said a prayer and asked for guidance. I began "journaling" my thoughts in order to clear my mind. Within 15 minutes, I began to receive answers. This guidance held incredible wisdom and peace—perfectly answering my questions and concerns. I knew these messages did not originate from me—language patterns were not my own, words that were not part of my vocabulary were used in perfect context, and topics of which I had very little knowledge were revealed in detail. The speed at which I received the messages was astonishing, compelling me to document their completion times.

I could not audibly hear these messages, I simply received feelings and visuals for each word. This made the process a bit difficult, but it became easier over time. The better I blocked out my mind and settled within my heart, the easier I could tune-in and receive. As soon as I would start to think about what I was receiving, the flow of the message would stop until I, again, settled my consciousness back into my heart.

At first, not realizing the magnitude of this gift or from where it was originating, I rarely devoted time to using this ability. I was so busy with the survival-state of life...and I was bothered that this "heartspeak" would be considered either weird or impossible by most of society. In fact, I only tapped into this ability 5 times within the first 2½ years. I had not realized it at the time, but this gift was the alarm that would eventually wake me up from sleepwalking through life.

April 2, 2009:

After 2½ years, I finally decided to stop ignoring this wake-up-call and utilize the gift I had been given. A friend who is also a counselor had encouraged me to do so, noting the beneficial wisdom and life-lifting spiritual qualities of the messages. That evening I received "God's Unfolding Truths", unaware that this would be the first of many chapters intended for a book.

May 22, 2009:

As I devoted time and focus to these messages, it finally occurred to me to ask who was providing this guidance, upon which I was told "Archangel Gabriel". Not having a formal religious background, I had no idea who that was until a bit of research revealed this "Messenger of God". I was amazed that what I learned of this archangel's essence, purpose and wisdom coincided with the guidance I had been receiving. At that point I began to realize the significance of what was happening.

This ongoing guidance opened my eyes, revealing truths and understandings. I was now able to see the purpose behind the hardship that my husband and I had endured, and had reassurance that there was a Greater Source of assistance, love and power beyond humanity's visible reality.

July 6, 2009:

Still struggling in a back-and-forth battle of trust in the not-so-visible versus the self-imposed "shoulds" of life, I was torn between finding a full-time job and devoting the summer to my children and part-time freelance work. Needing guidance, I asked and was told the following:

"You are not to fret...There is no need to seek any further...Set aside your worry for these remaining two months and let us see what changes transpire. Two months are doable without worry—one step at a time, one moment at a time. Live! Live! Live! Live each moment to the fullest through your heart and turn off your head. Watch your life unfold before your eyes."

I followed the advice and our lives continued to transform: my husband had settled into his "dream" job, his health issues improved, my feelings of depression had disappeared, and financially we were getting back on our feet. My life was unfolding and I was seeing it differently—seeing its journey and purpose, seeing my own significance, seeing the limiting misconceptions of mankind, and seeing the miracles of life.

July 20, 2009:

The few people that I shared these messages with were also benefiting and their lives were also transforming through their own shifts in perception and understanding. At that point I was told,

"You have been given this gift for a reason, a reason to share, a reason to flow with the greater goodness of God. It may stretch you to do so, but all must be stretched in order to grow. Trust, and the process will take place just as it is meant to. I, Archangel Gabriel, have been chosen to speak through you and deliver these messages from God. You have been chosen due to your insight and compassion into mankind's feelings and woes. Together we will make a team of mules, pulling at the souls of humanity, lifting them up the mountainous terrain until they stumble finally upon the answers that they have been seeking."

July 21, 2009:

That next day I witnessed a physical miracle, one that would provide me the much-needed confidence in order to more fully grasp and own this unbelievable gift. While I was tensely driving in traffic with my four children, I began to think about Archangel Gabriel's message from the previous night which instructively stated,

"Enjoy your seat and sit in it comfortably. What else is there but to enjoy all that you do and all that you have? There is wonderment and amazement in every moment if you choose to open your eyes and look around. Every lesson is a gift and every moment is to be taken with gratitude."

Immediately upon my relaxing into the moment, an extremely unusual rainbow-lit, spiral-shaped cloud appeared in the sky. It kept pace with our car for eight minutes then disappeared once we arrived at our destination. This miraculous sighting was a sign and a blessing to me—it could no longer be argued that these communications were simply my own thoughts. Witnessed by all five of us, this was evidence, through its timing and awesome, miraculous quality, that the received wisdoms and inspirations were from God. (The following chapter details and explains this sighting.)

July 24, 2009:

Three days later I was told that the messages were intended for a book:

"Your answers will come through the messages I speak—the answers of a lifetime, your lifetime—but these messages are universal and can benefit all of mankind. They need to be shared... Yes, a book it is, a format which will document my teachings... singing to the hearts of those that need answers. These gifts will arise and prosper into a magnificence—a journey that will launch a ship of heightened awareness...This can be accelerated through your help, through your translation of what I speak and what I need translated...Mankind is in need of these answers and you are the vehicle with which they can be delivered."

This pushed me beyond my comfort zone—presenting a book I did not write, especially one from such a miraculous source. It was overwhelming and draining at times, having such a daunting task...and encountering varying degrees of criticism and doubt from others. Saddled with my own doubts, I needed to reread messages in order to solidify understanding, break old patterns, and gain confidence. Archangel Gabriel assisted on numerous occasions by reassuring or gently reprimanding me...

"Cherish this gift and own it, love it, believe in it...Do not doubt this ability, do not doubt this gift. Yes, others can translate also, but there is a difference—one that spans and spreads, creating broken links and distortions as do whispers through tunnels of hollow branches...Stop disbelieving and see your gifts through my eyes, the eyes of God...This is your time, and the time is now to translate and to do so with confidence."

Pushing beyond my own insecurities, I chose to embrace this miraculous gift in order to share it with the world. From that day forward, I "tuned-in" and documented. During the process, I found the deeper understandings that I had been seeking, enabling me to "see" beyond the visible. These revealed truths have launched me into a journey of self-discovery and into my own power-of-being—a concept which, previously, had not been in my vocabulary!

This book is a compilation of Archangel Gabriel's messages, uncovering truths for the development and peace of humanity. The order in which the chapters are read is not important as each is independent and complete within itself, yet all relate to the whole. What is important is to realize that this is a process—a process of development and empowerment—a journey to learn and grow, and to unravel old patterns that have been established over years...decades...generations.

Every step that you take toward true understanding empowers you, bringing you closer to the realization of who you actually are and closer to the life that you are meant to live. You each have your gifts and significance to society. You simply need to uncover those gifts and shine with who you are in order to transform your life and the world.

~ PLEASE NOTE ~ The terminology in this book is of a traditional sense in its use of the name "God", as well as in its masculine genderization for both God and mankind. This is simply the language that flows through me and speaks most easily and clearly to a general audience. In actuality, according to Archangel Gabriel, "God is an energy of pure love, Light, power and strength and is neither male nor female."

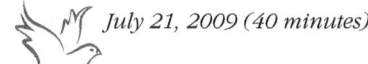 *July 21, 2009 (40 minutes)*

Visible Evidence: The Rainbow Light

On this day I witnessed a miracle that would give me the knowing confidence to launch this book of messages from Archangel Gabriel. I documented the details of the incident and later that night asked for insight.

At around 1 p.m., I was driving with my children through heavy traffic. I was tense with stress and began to think about the Archangel Gabriel message I had received the previous night which instructed me to live each moment with wonder and gratitude. I then decided to simply enjoy the drive and the beautiful day. As soon as I relaxed the tension out of my shoulders, my 9-year-old son yelled, "Oh my God, look at that! Look at that! Oh, my God!" At a stoplight, I was able to take a look. In the sky was a wispy spiral cloud with rainbow hues spreading in a triangular shape directly behind the wisps. It was miraculous and beautifully magnificent!

We continued to travel eastbound, taking a slight detour due to road work. The drive took an additional 5 minutes during which the cloud and rainbow-light remained south of us, keeping pace with our car. As we stopped at our destination, the cloud also stopped. We stood and watched for about a minute as it receded back (south) while strangely intensifying in color, and then it moved at a right angle (east) floating behind a massive white cloud—leaving us in awe. The day was calm and sunny and the sky was filled with large, thick clouds—all of which remained perfectly still. With no wind, this small spiral cloud had traveled for about 8 minutes in perfect pace with our car and then disappeared once we reached our destination. I had expected to see a crowd gathered in the store's parking lot, but other than the 5 of us, no one had even noticed.

This sighting was miraculous, incredibly beautiful, and quite amazing—like nothing I had ever seen before. I felt it was a sign and asked for insight. Following is Archangel Gabriel's response:

This was a miracle, a miracle of wonder and gratitude...a sign of hope and prosperity, love and light...a whisper from God...a miracle of creation and joy. It was a sign to you to watch for and notice the obvious, and beauty will shine through to tell a tale of sweet whisperings from the Heavens above. Watch and look toward the Heavens for your answers. There, miracles aspire to new births of love and Light, whispering messages of rainbow dreams and whirlwinds of hope—whisking away the humdrum relativity of hope gone awry. Watch and look forth into the coming Light where wonder and glory mix and mingle. Give rise to your spirit, settling your mind and relaxing your senses. Each day arises anew and each day aspires to a new thought or message giving vision and hope to those who open their eyes to see.

"You opened your eyes and experienced a gift from God, a message and sign of hope, an evidence that you are not alone and that miracles happen every day if you will just lift up your head to take notice."

You opened your eyes and experienced a gift from God, a message and sign of hope, an evidence that you are not alone and that miracles happen every day if you will just lift up your head to take notice. All other eyes were to the ground, no one else looking or seeing what revelation was set forth from Above for all to see. It was there for the looking and there for the taking...But who was open to actually see? You were and your children were. You were ready to see, to look, to listen and to learn. Not all are ready. Not all can see—see what is right before their eyes, see what there is to enjoy, see what there is to learn, and see what there is to experience.

"What a joy life can be if you simply allow it to be, and if you look for and notice the miracles of life..."

My, oh my, what a day you had—a glorious day of fun and friends and miracles and wonder. Every day can shine so brightly, as did this day. Simply allow it and it will come forth—come forth to knock your socks off with a click of the heels and a high-five. What a joy life can be if you simply allow it to be, and if you look for and notice the miracles of life which are all around you floating above your head.

> *"In the imagination lie the dreams of God. Make them into reality by believing in them, helping to transform the entire existence of mankind."*

Keep your head in the clouds and see what transpires—what dreams manifest into reality, for in the clouds lie imagination. And imagination spurts and sputters, creating growth from the raindrops and dew. Feel the whisperings, and fill your life with all of the wonders imagination can bring. In the imagination lie the dreams of God. Make them into reality by believing in them, helping to transform the entire existence of mankind.

> *"You are all here to grow and experience the beauty that is and can be for all to see..."*

Watch and learn from the beauty of nature, created from a palette of wonder and a brush of Light. Strokes filled with imagination paint a new picture of hope—igniting the flame that burns deep within your soul. Let the colors of nature wash over you and brighten the life that stirs within, lifting your hopes and aspirations and those of generations to come. You are all here to grow and experience the beauty that is and can be for all to see—a wonderment that is so tremendous that it gives way to a burst of sunlight and showers of fruitful rain, washing away the gullies that bind your hearts in pain.

> *"Nothing can compare with the beauty that God has set forth and has set into motion, swirling with the energy of the Universe. That energy and life resides within you all."*

Envelop life and its natural beauty, stopping to smell the roses, sniffing in the fruitful whispers of seasons gone by. Walk and touch the buds of life which bloom brightly all around you. These are the beautiful and bountiful gifts from God—those natural wonders that sparkle with all the colors of the rainbow. What is more beautiful? What is more natural?

Nothing can compare with the beauty that God has set forth and has set into motion, swirling with the energy of the Universe. That energy and life resides within you all. You are all to cherish it and utilize those God-given gifts, creating your own reality of bright, bountiful abundance and beauty. You all have that ability; you just have to see and be aware that it is there.

Just as that rainbow was overhead for all to see, only a select few chose to view its presence. It followed you and then disappeared, undocumented and unproven. There was no camera to capture the moment, but that moment will live forever in your hearts. You were God's witnesses. You saw His glory, and that was His gift to you. Take that gift and cherish it, knowing that it was sent for you—sent as a reminder and a message to you and your children that there is more out there than meets the eye. Revel and wallow in that glory, for that is the glory of the Kingdom to come. How awesome. How awe-struck you were. What wonder. What amazement. That is God and that is glorious!

> *"...there is more out there than meets the eye."*

When I have shared the Archangel Gabriel messages with others, I have experienced varying degrees of acceptance and belief. A loving friend of mine expressed her skepticism through the question, "Why are these messages coming from an angel rather than directly from God?" Below is Archangel Gabriel's response.

 *September 27, 2010 (14 minutes)*

God's Messages

Kathi, rest assured that I am always present—here to assist you in all that you need, all that you ask. You simply need to let go and let God.

I am of God, just as you are of God. You live and breathe God, and God lives and breathes you. We are all One—all of the same energy, wisdom, creation and Light. God speaks through me as He speaks through you. You are the essence of the Creator in all His magnificence and glory. His wisdom flows forth through me and through you. We are the vehicles for that translation—that translation of the Almighty's wisdom and grace.

---

*"The vehicle through which
God's message comes does not matter.
It is the message itself that is of the utmost importance."*

The vehicle through which God's message comes does not matter. It is the message itself that is of the utmost importance. The message simply must come into manifestation, and you are the vehicle through which it flows— the one who vibrates to the tune of His music. It does not matter that you are not God Himself...but you are of Him. You have allowed yourself and enabled yourself to be open to receive and translate His messages. That is the gift that you have given and that is the gift that you have received.

> *"The ultimate test, one which will determine whether or not these messages are of godly origin, is the vibration in which they resonate."*

Your ability to translate is a blessing, no matter how others may interpret it. Your receiving these messages is of utmost importance. Please do not allow others to alter your perspective and doubt yourself. Not all has to be explained. All that has to be known is the essence of the messages which spring forth from God the Almighty.

The ultimate test, one which will determine whether or not these messages are of godly origin, is the vibration in which they resonate. Are they for the greater good of mankind? Do they live and breathe out of love, truth and justice for the betterment of human society?...or do they harbor feelings of self-gratification and suppression, control and power over others? Those questions are the ones that must be asked when determining if an energy or message is godly or one that breeds negativity.

> *"It is the test to mankind: To give rise to his own power-of-being and choose to recognize his Creator, living as he is meant to in the cherishing of God and the brotherhood of all...or to turn his back and walk toward darkness."*

God's wisdom and energy flows through all—as He is the creator of all. All of creation is One, living and breathing out of this godly love. Through freewill, each and every being determines for himself whether he will live of-God, accepting the graces that have been granted to him... or whether he will shun what has been offered, denying the riches of his heritage. It is a choice that is made with every breath that is taken and with every beat of the heart—one that lifts the soul toward the Light or

> *"All can choose to live through divine wisdom, love and Light;*
> *and all can be a vehicle for the spreading*
> *of this God-energy. The desire must simply be there*
> *and the effort must be made..."*

away from it within that moment of time. It is the test to mankind: To give rise to his own power-of-being and choose to recognize his Creator, living as he is meant to in the cherishing of God and the brotherhood of all...or to turn his back and walk toward darkness.

All can choose to live through divine wisdom, love and Light; and all can be a vehicle for the spreading of this God-energy. The desire must simply be there and the effort must be made in order to radiate this godly Light—shaping and transforming society by living out of love and justice for all.

> *"We are all One—*
> *all of the same energy, wisdom, creation and Light."*

Encountering conflicting beliefs regarding "channeling" and this process, I asked the following questions for clarification and understanding:

~ Is this gift that I utilize considered "channeling"?
~ What is an angel and are you, Archangel Gabriel, male or female?
~ Are you of my soul family?

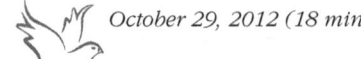

October 29, 2012 (18 minutes)

Defining Channeling, Angels & Souls

Kathi, my dear, you simply must settle within your heart, for that is how you "hear" me and receive the wisdom that flows forth from God the Almighty, Himself. Once you further hone this skill and gain the confidence that shall come due, you will be able to tap into this powerful energy of truth and reason within every waking moment of your life.

You are "channeling" in a sense, as you channel the truth and energy of God through your heart of purity and Light. You vibrate to that tune of God and can hone in to exactly where you need to be, keeping all other external influences at bay. You are not "channeling" per the definition described by humanity in which another soul or entity encompasses one's body and speaks through that physical being. That is quite different and can actually be dangerous as one gives up control over his own sense of self and being-of-life.

You are simply tapping into the Greater Wisdom of the Universe and are a forerunner of times to come. You have developed and honed a skill which you were born with but were unaware of its magnitude of magnificence until quite recently. You are not "channeling" as did those that encompassed the spirits of Ramtha and Seth, for example. Rather, you remain aware of your own essence and are simply encompassing the energy of God as voiced through me, Archangel Gabriel. Your heart hears the whispers of this truth and vibrates to the tune of its music. You are simply harnessing that wisdom, making it available to humanity—as that is your gift and that is your purpose.

I am the messenger of God—the energy that projects forth through love and Light of being. I have no gender, although the energy that emits forth and is the essence of me tends to be female in nature, as that is the energy that encompasses compassion and love, nurturing, and respect for the life force that resides in all. It is not the all-powerful, mighty, commanding energy that is considered to be more masculine in nature. It is rather, one built out of sensitivity and the essence of the Light of the soul—the essence of creation—that nurturing life-lifting energy that spins forth out of godly wisdom, love and Light.

> *"...an angel is an embodiment of God's energy created through the vision of mankind."*

I am not of your soul family. We are of similar essence when your heart is free and clear of harbored pain, yet that is also the essence of God. You are a child of God, as are all other humans of the Earth. That is the energy that created mankind, whereas an angel is an embodiment of God's energy created through the vision of mankind. Angels are energy that take on a personification in order to aid the understanding of humanity and put substance to that which is invisible to the human eye. We are available to all of humanity, one simply has to call upon that direction and guidance and be open to the receiving of the answer that is meant to shape release and understanding.

> *"Angels...are available to all of humanity, one simply has to call upon that direction and guidance and be open to the receiving of the answer that is meant to shape release and understanding."*

You are very closely related to the angelic kingdom, yet the energy of archangels is not of a soul-essence and is, therefore, not of anyone's soul family. The difference between the essence of a soul and the essence of an archangel is that a soul exists to reincarnate in order to come into perfection—to develop into all that is meant to be and intended by God in a seeking of love and truth. The essence of archangels is pure in love and Light and does not incarnate into human bodies. Their roles are to guide and teach, protect and aide, not learn and lift their own essence toward self-actualization and truth. Their energy is already of purity and strength, formed through the purity and strength of God Himself and does not need any shaping to obtain that purity.

"...a soul exists to reincarnate in order to come into perfection—to develop into all that is meant to be and intended by God in a seeking of love and truth."

"The essence of archangels is pure in love and Light and does not incarnate into human bodies. Their roles are to guide and teach, protect and aide, not learn and lift their own essence toward self-actualization and truth."

This chapter introduces Archangel Gabriel, summarizing the messenger's wisdom, teachings and guidance.

 *August 22, 2009 (50 minutes)*

Archangel Gabriel

I am Archangel Gabriel, the bearer of messages directed from God the Almighty. I have come through to you, Kathi, to guide mankind and give hope and direction to his growth and destiny through love and nurturing, wisdom and Light. I speak through you, and you translate from your heart my messages of wisdom and inspiration. Call forth upon your inner guidance and Light of your soul, and you shall "hear" my messages clearly and accurately—for the wisdom in your heart is a translation of the wisdom of God through me, Archangel Gabriel.

The remainder of the chapter and book speak to all of humanity.

You all must watch and learn, look and listen to the whisperings within your heart, mind and soul. Feel the messages that spring forth for the greater wisdom of mankind. I am available to offer assistance to all that seek answers, all that seek hope, and all that seek love and support from God the Almighty. He is there to nurture and love all of His children, nudging and guiding through life's tribulations. Growth offers the opportunity to reflect God's Light, launching the gifts that He grants upon his children.

All is meant to be shared. All is meant to be given. All is meant to be cherished. And all is meant to be offered in assistance to each other and

---

"All is meant to be shared. All is meant to be given. All is meant to be cherished. And all is meant to be offered in assistance to each other and mankind as a whole."

mankind as a whole. Nothing is meant to be squandered. Nothing is meant to be hoarded. Nothing is meant to be ruled. And nothing is meant to be burdened. You are all meant to live as One, with one purpose which is to serve each other and, therefore, to serve God—spreading His Light and lifting the world into enlightenment.

> *"Mankind is to walk hand-in-hand toward his full potential of being, shining forth and not blocking each other's Light."*

The world is to sparkle with joy and abundance and to radiate with gratitude and love. The Earth is to be showered with Light and growth, and to spring forth with life and wealth and prosperity. Mankind is to walk hand-in-hand toward his full potential of being, shining forth and not blocking each other's Light. You all must shine as One, illuminating the world and growing and giving together in moments of glory and servitude.

Watch in wonder and amazement as the Earth sings to a new tune and dances with glory as mankind shifts his consciousness and level of thinking to new heights of awareness—an awareness that emanates with God's abundance and magnificence, peace and love. Shine forth and shower the world with a radiance that springs from your inner being, spreading Light outward and upward to the Heavens, reflecting back and encompassing all in infinite wisdom, purpose and joy. Let go of the traps and boundaries that man has created, and release all to the wind—transforming the destiny of mankind. Stretch into the Light of God and allow His Light to settle the minds and worries of the Earthbound souls.

> *"Feel the dreams and callings from within and trust that these are guided with purpose and are sprung forth from a more powerful force…"*

Feel the dreams and callings from within and trust that these are guided with purpose and are sprung forth from a more powerful force—a calling from the Great Beyond. Listen to these callings, these whisperings of truth and justice. Do not fight these urges, but move forward with confidence and inner and outer guidance and direction. Let God be your shepherd and you shall not want, or suffer or fall—there is purpose to all.

> *"You each have your path and are not to be judged by others, nor are you to judge. Only you can know what is right for you by listening to your inner callings and the guidance from Above."*

Set forth on your path—your destiny—the one that calls and pulls at your soul. You each have your path and are not to be judged by others, nor are you to judge. Only you can know what is right for you by listening to your inner callings and the guidance from Above. Settle your mind and follow your heart, your soul, your spirit. Your heart is where the true answers and guidance lie, not within your mind, for the mind plays tricks and listens detrimentally to the gnawings and gnarlings of the past or the doubts and blabberings of others. The mind worries and struggles, playing games that spin out of control, trapping your soul in discontent and loss of time.

Watch for this misuse of time and precious resources, and let go of the past and future, for the power lies within the "now"—that moment of

> *"Watch for this misuse of time and precious resources, and let go of the past and future, for the power lies within the "now"—that moment of truth that rests at your fingertips in ever-presence."*

truth that rests at your fingertips in ever-presence. This presence is all that is necessary. It is all that is important, for nothing else has any real value to your present being or purpose. The only value that the past has, is that it got you to where you are at the present. The only value that the future has, is that it is where you will be as a result of what you do in the present. Therefore, the present is all that truly matters—all that truly is.

Utilize the present. Utilize every precious moment with conscious being, conscious living. That is what brings about miracles of awareness and Light and love, for to be truly present is to truly live, and to truly live is to truly create and nurture the being within—spreading your Light and reflecting the Light of God.

"...to be truly present is to truly live, and to truly live is to truly create and nurture the being within—spreading your Light and reflecting the Light of God."

"There is no glory in lost moments or in creating loss for others. There is no glory in blocking the Light of others or stomping out the life-force that God has granted."

Joy in life is what is intended and to live with joy is to create joy in others—nurturing your own soul while nurturing the souls of others. There is no glory in lost moments or in creating loss for others. There is no glory in blocking the Light of others or stomping out the life-force that God has granted. Cherish the gifts that God has bestowed upon you and upon the rest of His children. Do not take these gifts for granted and do not take your moments of being—of living—for granted. Cherish them, notice them, utilize them, and expand and spread them—igniting the spark within and launching an ever-extending chain of Light and miracles of God.

"There is no limit to the expansion of mankind's development unless limited thinking blocks that growth and expansion."

You have a purpose, as all beings do. Live that purpose and cherish and utilize the unique gifts and wisdom that you have been granted. There is no limit to the expansion of mankind's development unless limited thinking blocks that growth and expansion. Man is his own worst enemy, tripping himself up and knocking his brothers down in order to place himself on top. Lift yourself up—simply by following your own inner dreams, living with love and gratitude, trusting your purpose, following God's guidance, and living joyfully in each present moment.

Look not at another's path with disquieted resentments or jealousies, for another's path or purpose is not your own. It has no significance to your destiny—only does your ability to stay focused and to stay connected. Live with love and Light, direction and purpose, and you will find all that you are seeking. Your life will unfold before your eyes granting you joy and abundance, peace and Light-of-being.

"Look not at another's path with disquieted resentments or jealousies, for another's path or purpose is not your own. It has no significance to your destiny— only does your ability to stay focused and to stay connected."

Section II
Humanity's Misconceptions & Actual Truths

Mankind is a marvel and a must but has repressed itself and blocked its own good from prospering, causing things to roll out of control—twisting and turning the very world in which you live. You each have individualized lessons to learn and must come to realize the extreme power that you hold, and hold over others, through the connections that you make and the actions that you take.

You need to seek truth and take stands as individuals, realizing that when those stands are taken, results are shaped and hardships avoided. All must learn to band together and lift the Light of the world without fear of repercussion, for a silenced truth speaks to no one. Only when you give voice to truth, can it be heard and spread, enabling it to take root and grow strong and tall, protecting and sheltering in the belief and wisdom that it creates.

All must walk tall and live through the wisdom of God—the wisdom of truth and justice. This will enable mankind to flourish and prosper, creating the heavenly world that it desires.

"You have become trapped within the recesses of your own minds in a state of suppression, created by the norms of society and the limited thinking of mankind—not realizing your true full-potential...the potential for godly creation."

 March 2, 2010 (46 minutes)

The Power-of-Being

You all come to this Earth with a purpose which gets forgotten upon your birth into this realm of time and space. The gravitational pull of the Earth plays havoc with the freedom and flight of your soul and the energy that is meant to be lifted into the knowingness and enlightenment of God's wisdom and grace. You are all beings of Light meant to radiate forth with God's energy, dispelling negativity—unblocking the burdens of life.

You have become trapped within the recesses of your own minds in a state of suppression, created by the norms of society and the limited thinking of mankind—not realizing your true full-potential, for the potential within mankind is the potential for godly creation. The beings of mankind are, in actuality, beings of life, flowing with the essence of God in a radiant energy that lives and breathes out of love and Light. You have become burdened and trapped by your human thinking and have lost sight of your purpose and power which were known during your spiritual soul-state of existence before your birth into this lifetime.

Life is meant to give rise to your own power-of-being in a joyous creation and manifestation of love, Light and life, radiating forth in selfless giving, nurturing the Earth and its inhabitants. With the lack of awareness as to your own power-of-being—that which enables you to create the essence of your very existence—you give away that which you are, and turn over

"With the lack of awareness as to your own power-of-being—that which enables you to create the essence of your very existence—you give away that which you are, and turn over your power to others out of fear or lack of confidence."

your power to others out of fear or lack of confidence. This giving away of power keeps you trapped within pain, struggle and strife—unable to let your soul fly free and soar to new heights of development, blocking the path that you came to this Earth to travel.

The gift of life is a gift of discovery into yourself and your own power-of-being, the realization that everything is at your fingertips awaiting your manifestation. You are a child of God, given the gifts that God has bestowed upon you and the resources to put them into action—to put them into being. Do not turn your power away due to a lack of knowing...or fear...or concealed truths. Uncover who you are—a reflection of God's magnificence in all the brightness of Light and the beauty of love, able to do as you desire through this love and this life of creation and giving.

"You have boundless resources to call upon through angelic assistance and God Himself, but you must ask and you must be open to receive this guidance, support, wisdom and Light."

All will manifest once you come into this realization and open up to the wisdom of your heart which connects you to the Source of your creation and power—the wisdom of God and the Light and creative energy of the Universe. You have boundless resources to call upon through angelic assistance and God Himself, but you must ask and you must be open to receive this guidance, support, wisdom and Light. Do not block this almighty power and the essence of your soul due to a lack of understanding through human misconception of the powers-that-be. Seek a

> *"...all of humanity is One and must shine out of love and Light for all life in a nurturing, giving society that answers to all. Once this is done, there will be paradise on Earth and all negativity and suffering will be dispelled."*

higher understanding and wisdom that comes from the Source of all-knowing truth, and unravel your own truths.

Seek beyond human negativity and greed over power, which strive to suppress the realization of your individualized power-of-being. The truth-be-told is that all of humanity is One and must shine out of love and Light for all life in a nurturing, giving society that answers to all. Once this is done, there will be paradise on Earth and all negativity and suffering will be dispelled. This can only be accomplished through the rise of the love and Light of God through the individual. Each individual has free-will and each individual has freedom-of-choice in every moment of life. That choice can either reach upward, lifting you toward the flight of your soul, or it can drag and drain your energy, anchoring you in negativity and limited suppressed thinking.

> *"The enlightenment of each soul spreads its Light, helping to blanket the Earth in a powerful, lifting energy that smothers out the harmful, negative energy of the power-hungry & lost souls."*

The enlightenment of each soul spreads its Light, helping to blanket the Earth in a powerful, lifting energy that smothers out the harmful, negative energy of the power-hungry and lost souls. The more souls that become guided by the Light and awakened to their true power-of-being and the essence of God, the Lighter the energy of Earth will become—creating a world of truth, justice, love and Light in a joyous exchange that nurtures freedom, wisdom and support.

> *"Your heart is what enables feeling to flow and the true wisdom and all-knowing truths of God to enter your being and bring peace and freedom to your life…"*

You must release and free yourself from your mind's control and your perceived notions of how you view yourself and life on Earth. Those limited beliefs are what is suppressing you and chaining your soul. Your heart is what enables feeling to flow and the true wisdom and all-knowing truths of God to enter your being and bring peace and freedom to your life and life on Earth. All of the answers lie within—beating with the rhythm of God and resonating signals throughout your body.

All can be dispelled and released—anger, fear, lack, struggle, strife, poor health and pain—through the realization of your abilities and the calling upon of your Source of Creation, the energy of God. All can be overcome and no outcome is final. All has its purpose and all reaches beyond the visible—all bringing you to the realization of your own true-power and ability to create.

You are not your thoughts. You are not your pains. You are not your burdens. You are not your physicality. You are a being of Light utilizing a physical body. That physical body and your environment is under your

> *"You are not your thoughts. You are not your pains. You are not your burdens. You are not your physicality. You are a being of Light utilizing a physical body."*

> *"Once you understand your true Source of power and that help is ever-present, you will be able to shape your own life and reach beyond humanity's self-created limitations."*

control, within your own power of creation. Realize this power and dispel your pains and burdens, manifesting the life that you desire.

All is within your control, and all struggles and lessons direct you toward this realization. Once you understand your true Source of power and that help is ever-present, you will be able to shape your own life and reach beyond humanity's self-created limitations. This must stem from the individual—launching you into your own growth by unraveling the truths, mysteries and purpose for life. Through the awakening of individual souls, the love and Light will spread, lifting the burdens of all in a blanket of godly creation, beauty and abundance.

A shift in perception can shift your life, launching you into a flight of freedom that lifts your soul into the Light and love and power of God. That is the intention of life and its purpose—to bring humanity into this knowing and to the realization that love dispels all and that you are all One. Once there is true love for the individual self, it becomes clearly visible that there is no need to strike out to harm one another. A healing and empowerment of the self will enable a healing and empowerment of the whole of humanity and of Earth.

This book unravels the mysteries and misconceptions of what gives rise to the lack of true understanding which creates fear and anger, struggle and strife. The dispelling of these untruths, or lack of understandings, will enable you to see your true beauty and the essence of God—lifting your life into love and Light and the power-of-being. True understanding and forthright communication shall dispel all negativity, enabling peace and Heaven on Earth.

"True understanding and forthright communication shall dispel all negativity, enabling peace and Heaven on Earth."

♡

> *"One must face Truth within himself in order to grow and launch his life forward and away from stagnation and pain."*

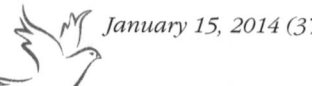

January 15, 2014 (37 minutes)

Truth with a Capital "T"

The topic of "Truth" is crucial to the survival of mankind, the evolution of the soul, and the development of humanity. Within Truth, life lessons are revealed and the path is shaped. If a soul or being does not face Truth, then how shall he unravel the mysteries of mankind—the mysteries of himself?

It is Truth that shall set each individual free, both on a personal level as well as a Universal one. One must face Truth within himself in order to grow and launch his life forward and away from stagnation and pain. The topic of "Truth" is complicated in that the mind twists and turns reality until one believes that his own truth is actual Truth as seen through the eyes of God. There is a mighty big difference between the reality of the mind and actual reality.

> *"The 'reality of the mind' is warped by many factors and fluctuates within the moment depending upon the current emotional state of the individual, as well as factors relating to past pain and history, personality and sensitivity level."*

> *"'Actual Truth' takes in all circumstance as well as internal & external motivation, presenting the reality of ALL that transpires."*

The "reality of the mind" is warped by many factors and fluctuates within the moment depending upon the current emotional state of the individual, as well as factors relating to past pain and history, personality and sensitivity level. Other factors play into that perception of truth—or interpretation of reality—which may be unbeknownst to that individual, such as leading events and circumstance, motivation from other sources, and outright actualization of reality. "Actual Truth" takes in all circumstances as well as internal and external motivation, presenting the reality of ALL that transpires. Truth with a capital "T" is that which is seen from all levels combined and is completely identified only through God Himself—that higher energy of love and honor, actualization and creation.

> *"The mind can twist and turn a situation in order for the ego of that individual to feel better or to avoid an undesired or uncomfortable action or circumstance."*

Each individual, in order to develop as quickly as possible and avoid erroneous behavior and action, must seek Truth with a capital "T"— unraveling the mysteries of the Universe and quieting the falsehoods and justifications of the mind. The mind can twist and turn a situation in order for the ego of that individual to feel better or to avoid an undesired or uncomfortable action or circumstance. That is detrimental to the soul, as the harnessing of actual Truth is a necessity in order to properly launch the individual and the world.

Based upon one's inner motivations, the ego can continue through an entire lifetime locked in the avoidance of reality and, thus, detrimentally spread that false reality outward to other individuals. That does not justly serve anyone. That does not serve that soul's highest good, and that does not launch that individual toward his greatest earthly potential—holding back the higher growth of the soul. When one reaches beyond the constraints of the mind and the limitations of the ego, that individual opens himself up to the realities of God, seeking beyond the limited human experience in an advancement to capture justice and good, love and

> *"Truth must be sought at all costs, as Truth is true reality."*

> *"True reality supersedes all limitations and launches one toward the manifestation of dreams into a world full of love and Light that can conquer all illusion and greed, self-righteousness and ego-based destruction."*

Light, enlightenment and soul development—launching himself toward paradise and also spreading that Light to lift and aid mankind.

Truth with a capital "T" will launch the individual away from lessons of hardship and toward the glory of a life guided by God. Truth must be sought at all costs, as Truth is true reality. True reality is much beyond what the typical human experiences, as mankind's limited thinking has limited his reality and falsified his life. True reality supersedes all limitations and launches one toward the manifestation of dreams into a world full of love and Light that can conquer all illusion and greed, self-righteousness and ego-based destruction.

Without Truth, the world would be dark and unfeeling, illusive and painful. Much of humanity experiences this cloud of darkness, as Truth is not enabled to prevail due to a lack of wisdom or to the allowance of darkness to rule. Truth with a capital "T" cannot be argued with, and an individual cannot successfully stand against Truth when justification and erroneous thinking are his means to a defense.

> *"Truth must not be replaced with illusion, as then the illusion will rule and those that buy into that illusion will suffer the consequences of that train of thought. Lessons will then manifest in order to steer that soul toward the realization of actual Truth..."*

Truth with a Capital "T"

Truth must not be replaced with illusion, as then the illusion will rule and those that buy into that illusion will suffer the consequences of that train of thought. Lessons will then manifest in order to steer that soul toward the realization of actual Truth, rather than the harboring of false reality or ill will. Lessons begin small and then become magnified and multiplied to the necessary level for that soul to open his eyes to reality. Once the lesson is learned and the Truth is obtained, that soul is released from the pull of that course and any pain and struggle that previously manifested to launch understanding and empathy with regard to the erroneous thinking and its consequential actions.

The more an individual seeks Truth rather than harboring a need to protect the ego or a sense of self-righteousness, the easier it will be for that individual to see clearly and feel what lies beneath the surface of mind-created reality. That individual will open up his world to one of True Knowing rather than harboring a need to protect ingrained behavior passed on by other humans who are ruled by mind-created illusion.

"The goal...is to strive to see through the eyes of God, seeing beyond illusion & deeper into the pains of others. When the Earth is covered with individuals that live through this Light of Knowing Truth, paradise will appear & no evil will survive—no illusion will deceive or repress, submerge or squash the goodness or Light of any life-form or situation."

The goal for each individual who graces the Earth is to strive to see through the eyes of God, seeing beyond illusion and deeper into the pains of others. When the Earth is covered with individuals that live through this Light of Knowing Truth, paradise will appear and no evil will survive—no illusion will deceive or repress, submerge or squash the goodness or Light of any life-form or situation. Purity will exist upon the Earth and God will prevail through the actions and intentions of each individual child of God.

Truth with a capital "T" is the end-all and the gateway toward paradise. It begins with the individual in a seeking of enlightenment, a reaching out to grasp ahold of reality in a determination to become one's best self. It magnifies and multiplies through the spreading of Truth in a stance for justice, voicing this Truth by speaking out for what is right and beneficial for the greatest good. The more individuals that do this, trusting that God shall support and provide, the quicker the Light will spread—transforming the energy of the Earth, knocking out the darkness and illusion of mind-created manipulation in order for paradise to appear.

"Compassion and understanding must always be sought and added to the equation when presenting Truth to another individual."

Please realize, this is not to say that Truth is to be spoken in an insensitive way. Compassion and understanding must always be sought and added to the equation when presenting Truth to another individual. Varying degrees of assertion are necessary due to the varying degrees of sensitivity and harbored pain within the individuals of humanity, as well as the varying degree of necessity for individualized Truths to be revealed.

To avoid Truth with a capital "T" in lieu of one conjured up by the ego, will only entrap and ensnare, dragging that individual toward a life of

"Each individual has choice through freewill, and that choice is backed by resulting transformations and manifestations. If one is experiencing struggle and strife— a manifestation of hell on Earth—then that is an indicator that actual Truth is not being noted or harnessed."

hell. Hell lives and breathes upon the Earth, just as does heaven. What do you choose for your life?...That is the question. All roads that shun the Truth of God—that Truth that lives and breathes out of true reality—lead to hell. God is an energy of good and love, Light and justice. Justice is served out through the granting of individual choice. Each individual has choice through freewill, and that choice is backed by resulting transformations and manifestations. If one is experiencing struggle and strife—a manifestation of hell on Earth—then that is an indicator that actual Truth is not being noted or harnessed. A careful examination of thought and action is highly recommended in order to steer away from that hell and shift toward a heavenly life of paradise, a path of clarity and vision.

Nothing is a clearer indicator of the level of energy or Truth that is being harnessed, than the resulting manifestations of positivity or negativity—lightness or darkness. These manifestations appear on an emotional, spiritual and physical level indicating the level of harmony through which one lives.

The Truth is that each individual creates his own reality and can shift that reality through the level of Truth that he seeks. Is one living at an ego-based, mind-created level or at a level worthy of God? Seek Truth and you shall be set free. It may take some work in order to unravel the mystery of your own thoughts and patterns of behavior, yet with each step that you take toward actual Truth, you will free up your life, moving toward paradise while also aiding the surrounding world.

"...each individual creates his own reality and can shift that reality through the level of Truth that he seeks."

"Seek Truth and you shall be set free."

> *"Through the harboring of negative energy, one brings about darkness as the Light of God is shunned, opening up that individual to a pathway of pain and struggle."*

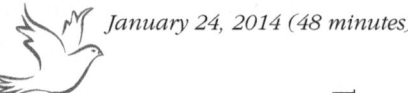 *January 24, 2014 (48 minutes)*

Energy

Lift your energy to fly free from the constraints of the Earth, the trouble that humanity drags itself into. You are a precious child of God and you must come to understand your true self, not that self that has been minimized by mankind through the harboring of ill thought or ill will. Mankind has enlocked himself within struggle and strife due to the harboring of his ego rather than the harnessing of the energy of God.

It is not mankind's right to seek to control or shun humanity—that which God created. It is God's will that mankind learn to see beyond the oppressive-mind, which is controlled by an overbearing ego, and to reach into the grace of God to capture the beauty and essence of life. Humanity has repressed and hoarded, shunned and stricken down the very souls of his brethren—some through outright cruelty and some through manipulation in order to serve a need within the self. That is not just, and that will bring about lessons of pain in order to launch growth.

These actions harbor negative energy and shun the magnificent godly energy of love and Light, truth and justice. Through the harboring of negative energy, one brings about darkness as the Light of God is shunned, opening up that individual to a pathway of pain and struggle. When one seeks to harm, he lets his own guard down and is susceptible to energies of a dark nature—those energies that are considered evil or, in traditional religious terms, of-the-devil.

> *"With every choice of thought or action, one brings about either energy of a good nature or that of an opposing force, reflecting that of positivity or negativity."*

> *"Energy is attracted in a just way, as what is released out to the world through intention is drawn back in through consequential Universal action. The just results of thought and action may appear instantaneously or over time through the administration of lessons."*

With every choice of thought or action, one brings about either energy of a good nature or that of an opposing force, reflecting that of positivity or negativity. Energy is attracted in a just way, as what is released out to the world through intention is drawn back in through consequential Universal action. The just results of thought and action may appear instantaneously or over time through the administration of lessons.

The sole (or soul) purpose for incarnation upon this Earth is to bring about godly development through humanity. All is created to bring about learning and just-thinking, administering love to lift the Light of the world in order to create paradise. Each soul of God has a predestined role to play out which is to launch understanding and development through the granting of energy. When one truly understands that he, himself, is responsible for his own circumstances, whether they be peaceful and godly or negative and dark, he will be able to effectively launch his life and help launch the lives of those around him.

> *"The sole (or soul) purpose for incarnation upon this Earth is to bring about godly development through humanity."*

One brings about energy, which manifests in the physical, through the thoughts that he harbors within. The mind rules when the heart-guidance of God is blocked. The energy of the Earth is heavy, and it is difficult to see with clarity that which lies beyond the visible. Mankind lives mainly through five senses. Yet to evolve to the level that God intends, mankind must lift his vision and make keen all his senses—those senses that are beyond the normal comprehension of mankind. Those senses, like the typical five, are granted by God and must be developed through the understanding of the godly nature of the Universe—one created out of energy and one that spins truths out of that energy.

> *"If one ignores the signals and manifestations of dark energy, then he will further sink into despair, manifesting deeper pain and harsher lessons."*

When one harbors an energy of darkness, he will further attract and magnify that darkness. When one harnesses an energy of Light, he will further brighten his life and lift his vision to true understanding, and the godly gifts of the Universe will be presented. Only can these gifts come if one is truly walking that higher road to truth and enlightenment. Otherwise, that which appears is a reflection of the harbored energy within and its resulting gifts of hardship. Those gifts of hardship are meant to signal that individual so that he can redirect his path toward one of enlightenment and godly manifestation. If one ignores the signals and manifestations of dark energy, then he will further sink into despair, manifesting deeper pain and harsher lessons.

> *"Even the smallest snag within life is an indicator that the energy is not clear or that thinking is not truthful or lifted toward the vision of God."*

> *"One does not need to worry about the punishment or justness of others. That shall be taken care of by that individual himself and the godly ways of manifestation."*

All must walk a fine line toward the realization of truth, noting all manifestations of energy. Even the smallest snag within life is an indicator that the energy is not clear or that thinking is not truthful or lifted toward the vision of God. One does not need to worry about the punishment or justness of others. That shall be taken care of by that individual himself and the godly ways of manifestation. All one need do is to focus upon the purity of his own heart and the truths of his own thoughts and actions, doing what is within his own power to do. Truth must be sought at all costs in order to harness the proper energy, or that individual will suffer the consequences. All must strive for purity of intention—purity of motivation. When one is at a level of godly purity, he seeks, within that moment, to obtain the best results for humanity's highest good or the highest good of the situation. He is not compelled in motivation to serve an ego-driven need.

> *"When God's children can rise above the grasp of the Earth's gravitational pull, the sense of powerlessness in the downtrodden, and the reign of ego in the power-hungry, lifting their energy to capture the wisdom and energy of God, then no evil shall prevail as all will be visible—all will be transparent."*

The goal of God is that all of His children develop to a level in which the greatest good of humanity is continually served through love and Light and the power-of-being. When God's children can rise above the grasp of the Earth's gravitational pull, the sense of powerlessness in the downtrodden, and the reign of ego in the power-hungry, lifting their energy to

> *"Each step toward positivity and truth will bring about an increased energy of Light, pushing away the darkness."*

capture the wisdom and energy of God, then no evil shall prevail as all will be visible—all will be transparent. The senses and vision-through-the-heart shall open, revealing the All-Knowing aspect of God in a radiant energy of love and Light and the power of absolute truth.

All of humanity is capable of achieving this level of realization, launching into enlightenment and the obtaining of paradise upon Earth. This can be achieved for each individual within his current lifetime of existence, as long as he harnesses and directs his energy toward that of godly truth and actualization. Some individuals are more aware of true reality, as they do currently see beyond the visible in a heightened intuitive awareness, able to read the energy that lies beneath surface illusion. Yet all beings can train themselves to do so. Each step toward positivity and truth will bring about an increased energy of Light, pushing away the darkness. Each step toward the development of one's highest potential—that of godly magnificence—will lift that individual away from the entrapments of the Earth's energy and humanity's oppressive nature.

> *"Meditation and energy-work, body movement and proper nutrition, clear communication and the speaking of truth, and grasping for godly awareness rather than that simply served by the ego, will all help launch an individual's life toward the realization of paradise."*

Meditation and energy-work, body movement and proper nutrition, clear communication and the speaking of truth, and grasping for godly awareness rather than that simply served by the ego, will all help launch an individual's life toward the realization of paradise. Paradise is a state that is untouched by the negative. It is a state of purity and grace that is guided by the energy of God which is that of love and Light, and the power of beauty and strength, truth and knowing—a capturing of the essence of all in a clear definitive of action and result. It is the ability to see all that TRULY is—all that lies beyond the surface of despair—in order to shape the energy of harbored pain and unjust action into one that lifts toward understanding and godly manifestation. It is the energy of the angelic— one that soothes and comforts, grants and magically manifests beyond the limitations of the currently typical, human experience. It is an art of living that is meant to be achieved by all.

"All that prevents the realization of paradise is humanity's stubborn refusal to see that which TRULY is, that which lies beyond a damaged sense of self & an overbearing ego that strives to protect. That 'protection' is actually detrimental if truth is shunned & 'fear' is allowed to rule & control."

All that prevents the realization of paradise is humanity's stubborn refusal to see that which TRULY is, that which lies beyond a damaged sense of self and an overbearing ego that strives to protect. That "protection" is actually detrimental if truth is shunned and "fear" is allowed to rule and control. There is no actual fear other than that of an instinctual nature. What humanity often labels as "fear" is simply a mind-created illusion that keeps one from venturing beyond the comfortable or that which has been erroneously taught to the individual through limited thinking.

"Thought is a discipline that shapes the energy around. One must direct his thought to the obtaining of actual truth…in order to steer away from that which can ensnare in a negative way."

One must strive to reach beyond the visible, open up his heart to allow the voice of God to come through, and seek to only harness the energy of God. All other energy shifts one toward the negative. One cannot harness both within an instant. Thoughts either gravitate toward the positive or negative…or there is no thought at all. The state of non-thought can be blissful or detrimental, as that being will harness that which he is susceptible to due to the energy that he has attracted. Thought is a discipline that shapes the energy around. One must direct his thought to the obtaining of actual truth—truth seen through the all-knowing, vantage point of God—in order to steer away from that which can ensnare in a negative way.

"To quiet the mind enables the heart to open and the messages of God to flow through."

There are disciplines of the mind that must be practiced so that the workings of the mind do not spin out of control and ensnare in a downward spiral. One must learn to watch his thoughts and stop them when they take over, quieting unnecessary chatter. To quiet the mind enables the heart to open and the messages of God to flow through. With practice and discipline, one will learn to properly identify which thoughts are of the mind and which are of a Higher Energy. "Truth" is the key to all, and truth shall lead to enlightenment and the recognition of the level of energy that is present or being presented.

Some techniques utilized to quiet the mind are sleep, meditation, qigong and any other form of body movement in which focus is utilized to bring

"The gift of nature is one of the quickest ways to relax into the energy of God if one can simply observe and cherish—noting the magnificence and miracle that have been granted through the highest form of energy."

> *"The key is to harness a state of being and awareness that captures the true essence of reality, rather than to become ensnared within the false-reality of the mind which is limited by conditioned thinking and influenced by the presence of external energies."*

in Light or still the chatter of the mind. The gift of nature is one of the quickest ways to relax into the energy of God if one can simply observe and cherish—noting the magnificence and miracle that have been granted through the highest form of energy. Communication in a clear, empowered way will also rid the mind of harbored chattering. A few minutes of proper verbal release will release one's dwelling within the mind and will also open up an individual to alternative perspectives—shedding Light upon the actual truth of a situation. The key is to harness a state of being and awareness that captures the true essence of reality, rather than to become ensnared within the false-reality of the mind which is limited by conditioned thinking and influenced by the presence of external energies.

This book launches one toward the understanding of how to open up the heart in order to capture truth and understanding and the energy that shall lead one into paradise.

> *"Paradise is a state that is untouched by the negative. It is a state of purity & grace that is guided by the energy of God which is that of love & Light, & the power of beauty & strength, truth & knowing—a capturing of the essence of all in a clear definitive of action & result."*

> *"Man has suffered much and continues to suffer as he is not open to the wisdom of the heart."*

 *September 11, 2009 (59 minutes) – Anniversary of 2001 terrorist attacks*

The Plight of Mankind

I offer to you my wisdom on the plight of mankind. Man has suffered much and continues to suffer as he is not open to the wisdom of the heart. Mankind as a whole has gotten caught up in the greed of the Universe rather than the energy that lifts it to shine forth in glory for all. You are all meant to share and assist, rather than to squander and lock away your hearts in order to protect yourselves, shutting out others who walk along your paths. Open up to each other and the Light of God, and your path shall also open up to gloriously bright, sunshiny days that sparkle with life.

> *"The journey is far more enjoyable if it is shared in harmony... It can be long and lonely if you choose to walk alone."*

Allow the Light of God to enter into your being, brightening every step you take along your winding road, and you will be lifted to new heights—for in the road ahead lies new growth and birth when it is traveled with an open heart, encompassing the whole of Earth and its inhabitants. Cherish this life in all, surrendering to the pull of the Earth's gravity, giving way to the wonder that is offered to mankind through the trials and tribulations of the journey. The road widens and narrows; it straightens and twists—all in a journey of discovery. The journey is far more enjoyable if it is shared in harmony with your brothers of the Earth. It can be long and lonely if you choose to walk alone.

> *"Do not look at the journey as a task or burden,
> but rather as an adventure to cherish in the knowingness
> that you are a co-creator with God and your brothers,
> designing and shaping a glorious world to come."*

In the midst of this journey of life comes change and growth that abounds with the ever-unfolding discovery of the Universal truths, which are presented in a sequence of events and adventures opening up your world to a multitude of opportunity. Look to this opportunity of life as a gift from God that springs forth your growth from within. It is an opportunity to seek and discover your soul and its purpose.

Do not look at the journey as a task or burden, but rather as an adventure to cherish in the knowingness that you are a co-creator with God and your brothers, designing and shaping a glorious world to come. Enjoy the journey and all of the characters that you meet along the way. Share of yourself and of your brothers, learning from each other and assisting each other along the path.

> *"Man has created his own struggles and strains
> through the hardened or distant relationships that he fosters
> and the burdens that he places against his fellow brothers."*

The plight of man has been prolonged and burdened by the apprehension and fear that blocks the road to riches. Man has created his own struggles and strains through the hardened or distant relationships that he fosters and the burdens that he places against his fellow brothers. You are meant to live as One and not to divide and conquer each other, destroying your villages and pillaging your opportunities. You are losing the battle against yourselves, and you will destroy your own lives in return, delaying your progress and stomping out the very livelihood that you create.

> *"There is plenty for all and plenty more can be created with the combined resources and Light of each other. The combining of all resources and all of mankind will complete the picture, creating a whole that far exceeds the sum of the divided parts."*

Cherish the gifts of God that lie within each others' souls and that shine through each others' eyes. Do not cloud your vision and block your sight by squelching out the Light that is meant to shine forth and shine together. You all must live as One and lift mankind to new heights, trusting the goodness that resides in all, and pulling forth the beauty and joy that is meant to shine and spring forth from all of the inhabitants of Earth. Pull together and fight no more. Work toward the good of all and no longer subdivide in a quest to prove superiority over each other. There is plenty for all and plenty more can be created with the combined resources and Light of each other. The combining of all resources and all of mankind will complete the picture, creating a whole that far exceeds the sum of the divided parts.

Even within individual countries, man is divided and subdivided, trying to squash and conquer all for which it stands. Once divided, you may fall and you may never stand again. Watch where you choose to walk and watch what you choose to battle for or against. Are you fighting the cause?...or simply fighting each other for the sake of disagreeing, or saving face, or proving superiority? A divided house cannot stand and will soon crumble into dust. Out of the buried ashes then must rise a new species that can continue forth into the progress of the world that God intends. Do not destroy yourselves and the glory that is meant to be.

Simply live forth with love and Light, snuffing out the greed and insensitivity and strife of the world. Take heart and learn to live a new kind of life filled with cohesion and servitude toward all of mankind. Respect each other and your differences, for in difference comes diversity that

> *"Respect each other and your differences, for in difference comes diversity that can lift your world into...complete abundance and joy, nurturing and respect, creativity and wonder..."*

can lift your world into an all-encompassing display of rainbow-hued Light and vision that shines forth, creating a world of complete abundance and joy, nurturing and respect, creativity and wonder—an awe inspiring world that is brighter than any other world of this day. Watch in glory as you band together as a brotherhood...or watch in agony as you crumble in despair, wiping out your species in a tumultuous heat of rage.

> *"You are all equal in the eyes of God and must also remain equal in each other's eyes."*

Quiet your souls and soothe your minds and together create a world designed upon the wings of change. Change the direction of your world through the change of your own heart—accept and nurture the Light that shines within each and every soul that has been granted the cherished life that he lives. You are all equal in the eyes of God and must also remain equal in each other's eyes. You have no right to force or to judge, to hinder or to hamper, based upon the beliefs within your own warped or burdened minds. Your minds have been brainwashed and hindered by your past and generations past, but you all have the opportunity and the responsibility to lift those burdened minds out of the despair and fear.

Lift your minds and hearts and the souls of mankind by opening up to each other and the Light of God, trusting in the beauty and intelligence, wisdom and inner knowing of mankind as a species—and you shall suffer no more. Now is the time. Now is the time for change and transformation of your world. Lift yourselves out of this turmoil by supporting your brothers and those in need.

> *"No longer hinder the progress of those that set forth to launch the good of society, but help to free your world through your support and contribution. Determine your actions based upon what is best for the greater good of mankind..."*

No longer hinder the progress of those that set forth to launch the good of society, but help to free your world through your support and contribution. Determine your actions based upon what is best for the greater good of mankind, not through selfish means of satisfying a need that lies restless within your own being. Stretch beyond that simple need and seek a broader vision—one that spans the horizons and transforms your world, co-creating the bigger picture of magnificent beauty that nurtures the Earth and all of its inhabitants. No longer be lost to your soul's anguish and mistaken past history. Move in a different direction, one of glory and God-given riches equally shared and granted to all, as it should be and is meant to be.

> *"Now is the time to make a difference. Make that difference now before there is no difference to make, before there is no world to take, before there is no love left, and before there is no man to forsake."*

Suffer no more in anguish and pain, ripping and shredding at your brothers' doorsteps. Walk away. Turn the other cheek, for in forgiveness lies comfort, and in fortitude lies confidence in the goodness of mankind's Light of knowing spirit—the spirit of God. Walk hand-in-hand and you shall no longer walk in fear, or in grief, or in greed, or in lack. Now is the time to make a difference. Make that difference now before there is no difference to make, before there is no world to take, before there is no love left, and before there is no man to forsake.

The Plight of Mankind

Do not continue to squander away the riches of the world for your own gain and power, comfort and strength. That is not your right and it is not your right to wield power over the heads of your fellow brothers. Try and you shall NOT succeed, as God is your witness and He is on the side of those that serve Him and the Light of his fellow brothers.

You are to serve mankind and kindle his spirit which will, in turn, kindle your own. Do not try to stomp out the flames of your brothers, for in that stomping, you smother your own life and calling within. Walk together and lift the world to where it is meant to be—shining in the Light of God and the greater vision of mankind.

"You are to serve mankind and kindle his spirit which will, in turn, kindle your own. Do not try to stomp out the flames of your brothers, for in that stomping, you smother your own life and calling within."

> *"Weave your significant path forth, choosing
> to contribute consciously to the greater good of mankind—
> helping to launch the world toward a beautiful vision
> of artistry and truth, justice and wisdom."*

 *September 6, 2009 (46 minutes)*

Your Significance in the Interwoven World

Look deep within to discover the truths that lie in justice—the justice of mankind and the Earth—the Universal laws that stretch beyond the human mind and sing to the hearts and souls of life and God. Seek beyond your mind and unblock the vision that holds you back from your dreams and wonders, for in wonder comes magic and mystery defined by truth and being.

Wash away the cobwebs of your mind and clear a path to new discovery and growth, one which will unfold into the dreams of tomorrow and the visions of future generations to come. All is to be seen with the heart and awakened to the soul. All is meant to be set forth and laid before mankind in a gesture of goodwill to man and devotion to woman. Take heart and whisper the truths that bring justice to all. Those truths lie locked within your very being and are rooted within your soul. They span the Universe and are ever-present within the vast encompassment of life itself.

God is your witness and is always with you. He seeks not enslavement and wants not sacrifice. He simply desires development of the soul and compassion and servitude for life itself and liberty for all. Help to heal this in the humans of the Earth and lift the development of your own being as well

> *"God...seeks not enslavement and wants not sacrifice. He simply desires development of the soul and compassion and servitude for life itself and liberty for all."*

as that of mankind as a whole. Life unfolds and unwinds in a road map of opportunity that launches society, creating a picture-perfect web of wonder that weaves out God's plan. You all take part in the bigger picture of things to come—of the Earthly movement of time and the development of the Universe. You are all here to accomplish what you had set out to do before your births into this human existence. Delve deeply within to pull forth that vision into your mind's eye and clarify, once again, this purpose that at one time was so visible and apparently necessary and crucial to the whole intricate pattern of life. Feel the mystery of life's callings and stretch forth into your deeper being to guide and pull you toward that realization.

> *"There is limitless power and knowing that guides mankind and helps pattern out this plan, but there is freewill that reigns within each human soul. All must give permission and all must journey at his own pace."*

Your path winds and is interwoven with the other inhabitants of the Earth, and all paths connect to form a road map of wonders that journey forth to create a new richer, more fulfilling life as a whole. Set forth on your path with vigor and strength guided by vision from the Great Beyond. There is limitless power and knowing that guides mankind and helps pattern out this plan, but there is freewill that reigns within each human soul. All must give permission and all must journey at his own pace. In order to complete the bigger, greater picture that mankind weaves, each soul must complete his own path arriving at his destined station in due time. Within that station is a platform for life and a purpose

> *"When one lifts his spirit to join his brothers, he creates a brighter more glorious picture of interwoven design and Light. When one chooses not to shine forth but to pull away... he leaves a void or hole in the greater vision of mankind."*

that is crucial to the life that is destined to arrive there. The weavings and windings of the paths of humanity as a whole connect to or bypass the path of the destined body, working with or avoiding that place of destiny. The greater picture is altered for all of mankind with the contribution or avoidance of that destined soul.

When one lifts his spirit to join his brothers, he creates a brighter more glorious picture of interwoven design and Light. When one chooses not to shine forth but to pull away from his brothers, he leaves a void or hole in the greater vision of mankind. That void must be worked around and patched and patterned with Light. It then takes a greater energy from the conforming souls to lift and heal those around and those who shall enter in the generations to come.

> *"You all play a crucial role—a place that holds special importance and significance to your being and your Light... It does not matter what work your hands toil at but rather how your heart reaches and connects with those around and those in need."*

> *"Your sensitivity to the plight of man is what pulls at the heartstrings of your being; it is what lifts you to new heights of development and enlightenment."*

Your Significance in the Interwoven World

You all play a crucial role—a place that holds special importance and significance to your being and your Light. Dance in this Light and play a tune that echoes forth into the rhythm of man's being and place in the future of the world. It does not matter what work your hands toil at but rather how your heart reaches and connects with those around and those in need. Your sensitivity to the plight of man is what pulls at the heartstrings of your being; it is what lifts you to new heights of development and enlightenment. Cherish the beauty in love and gratitude. Feel the pains of those around you and answer the prayers of those in need. Do not numb your mind and heart to the feelings and callings of mankind. That is not the purpose of living. That is contrary to how man is meant to develop and grow forth into the Light of God.

With sensitivity comes growth and transformation of the soul, a transformation that carves a new path into a deeper, more developed meaning and cherishing of life and God and His wonders of beauty and miracles of the heart—for the heart can heal all the pains of the past and truths gone awry. Feed your soul with the gifts of the heart and the gifts of God, for the true gifts of Light are the gifts of love and servitude. These shall lift your life and spirit into a miraculous, joy-filled adventure of peace and protection, nurturing and abundance. Travel your path—one that lifts you and shows you the way into your heart and the hearts of your brothers—and your path will branch out leading you to a new life of love and joy. That path will help form a more magnificent picture, lifting all of mankind to unsurpassed heights of development.

---

*"The past holds you back from future vision
when it blocks the Light of your heart.
The past brings you gloriously away from future suffering
when it launches you beyond repeated mistakes—
transforming the soul of mankind."*

Do not be afraid to shine forth projecting for all to see, lighting your own path and brightening the world's painted picture of glory—for in glory is God, and in God is love with no lack and no more suffering of the past. The past holds you back from future vision when it blocks the Light of your heart. The past brings you gloriously away from future suffering when it launches you beyond repeated mistakes—transforming the soul of mankind. Weave your significant path forth, choosing to contribute consciously to the greater good of mankind—helping to launch the world toward a beautiful vision of artistry and truth, justice and wisdom.

"Do not leave your mark by leaving a void where you were meant to shine."

Design and fashion a transformative picture of joy that nurtures all of mankind, creating a world of love and Light that sparkles with the individual choice of each and every heart-lit soul. Do not leave your mark by leaving a void where you were meant to shine. Share with your brothers your greater self, reflecting the Light of God through the path that you weave out of giving and caring connection to the brotherhood of mankind. Live through the Universal truths of justice, projecting forth out of love and Light and appreciation for life itself. Look to God for guidance and your steps will not falter. They will carry you to your destined self and into a world lit with magnificence and glory. Oh, what a miraculous world this will be once it sparkles with the flames of each and every soul, creating a glorious picture that radiates with God's love and Light-of-being.

"Look to God for guidance and your steps will not falter. They will carry you to your destined self and into a world lit with magnificence and glory."

During a religious man's skepticism regarding this material, he requested that I ask Archangel Gabriel whether or not I should read the Bible. I asked for insight into this, as well as the religious view that "in order to enter Heaven, one must believe Christ is God Himself or God's only son".

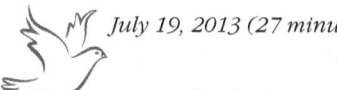 *July 19, 2013 (27 minutes)*

Humanity's Damaging Limitations of God

You must always settle within your heart in order to receive with purity and grace the words of God the Almighty. Simply live your life with goodness and grace in order to capture the essence and energy of God.

"When an individual can calm the chatter of the mind in order to hear the whispers of his Creator, then that child of God shall be set free in order to live a life of just reward."

God is an energy of love and Light, one that does not harness a rigidity for what His children are to do. Each must choose for himself what is accurate and just. This wisdom whispers through the heart and is meant to guide each individual forth toward truth and justice, peace and love. When an individual can calm the chatter of the mind in order to hear the whispers of his Creator, then that child of God shall be set free in order to live a life of just reward.

God whispers to the soul and is evident in many doctrines, and appears on a daily basis in the miracles of the Earth. The Bible is an important tool that has led many men forth, yet that is not the only vehicle that represents the word of God. God's word appears everywhere, and can flow forth through each individual soul if allowed and nurtured by that individual.

> *"God is an all-loving presence that makes no judgment and does not unfairly punish. Punishment is of man's own creation and manifests in the form of lessons..."*

It is the intention of God that each of His children learn to discern for himself what truly is just and fair, peaceful and loving—learn to discern what is of God and what is of His antithesis. God is an all-loving presence that makes no judgment and does not unfairly punish. Punishment is of man's own creation and manifests in the form of lessons—lessons that nudge that individual back on-track and into the loving arms of God. God does not judge His children. He simply desires that all live and do as He does—live and do in order to create a world of paradise that has no lack, no anger, no pain and no unjust action to harm the brotherhood of mankind.

When individuals can freely live without judgment, then anger will disappear, fear will be banished, and all will live out of faith and kindness, justice and peace. One need not read the Bible if one has a heart of purity and Light. One must simply strive for truth and justice, love and kindness. If one chooses to gather information from other sources, then so be it. The Bible is not for all. It is simply a doctrine that has recorded many accounts of God's will. God's will does not stop with the Bible and should not be limited to that resource.

> *"God has no limits and should not be held in that regard. Man himself has placed limits upon God and has twisted God's very word due to his own harbored prejudices."*

What kind of God simply disappears after presenting one gathering of information to one group of people?...A very limited one. God has no limits and should not be held in that regard. Man himself has placed limits upon God and has twisted God's very word due to his own harbored prejudices.

> *"If limits are placed upon God,
> that individual will limit his own life, bringing with it
> prejudices that reside within until that soul learns otherwise
> through lessons that expand his vision."*

It is up to man to decide for himself, on an individual basis, what it is that God truly intends. That individual decision will determine the outcome of that individual's life. If limits are placed upon God, that individual will limit his own life, bringing with it prejudices that reside within until that soul learns otherwise through lessons that expand his vision.

To say that one must read the Bible in order to understand life and understand God is erroneous, as that is a limited view stereotyping all souls of God. There are varying degrees of development within the race of humanity, and one pathway is not necessary or right for all. Many souls of the Earth have no exposure or access to the Bible or to Christ's teachings. Is it fair to say that those souls will be damned to a life that has no access to the Kingdom of their Creator?...That circumstantial outcome would demonstrate an unjust and unfair God, and God is no such thing. God is an energy of purity and Light, and cannot be limited and diminished in that way.

God is evident in the teachings of today, just as He is in the teachings of ancient civilizations. God flows throughout the world, just as does His opponent. It is up to mankind to determine what is truly just and

> *"It is up to mankind to determine what is
> truly just and fair, and to allow others to live freely
> without wielding unjust power of control.
> Freedom is the answer, and the flight of the soul is goal."*

fair, and to allow others to live freely without wielding unjust power of control. Freedom is the answer, and the flight of the soul is goal. What is of importance is simply the essence of the individual and the purity of his heart. Does one strive to love and to give and to stand for truth and justice?...or does one strive to force his own views and suppress his fellow brethren?

"Where there exists God in purity of form, there exists no human ego."

"It is not man that has the answers, it is the energy of God that flows with the Highest Truth. It is the job of mankind to seek this truth with an open mind and an open heart in order to open up the gates of paradise."

Where there exists God in purity of form, there exists no human ego. It is not man that has the answers, it is the energy of God that flows with the Highest Truth. It is the job of mankind to seek this truth with an open mind and an open heart in order to open up the gates of paradise. Heaven and hell reside upon the Earth. The energy that each individual harnesses determines what that individual will experience in his current lifetime.

All individuals have access to God, and no one is shunned from entering God's Kingdom, for to limit the life or fate of an individual based upon preferential treatment or prejudice is unjust, and God is not unjust. It is mankind himself that has limited and delayed his own progress. Mankind has the ability of godly manifestation, just as Jesus did. All are God's children and all are meant to do as Jesus did—to walk on water and lift their lives to the level of godly creation. It is simply mankind's limited thinking and the twisting of the word of God that has manifested into suffering and delay.

The Bible is instructive in its teachings, yet is subject to much misinterpretation, as is all material. Simply the tone in which one reads can twist the intent of a writing. Each individual soul must feel through the heart while blocking out the entrapments of the mind, for the heart is what receives the purity and grace of God, revealing the truth that is meant to shine through.

"All are God's children and all are meant to do as Jesus did—to walk on water and lift their lives to the level of godly creation. It is simply mankind's limited thinking and the twisting of the word of God that has manifested into suffering and delay."

> *"The more that understanding is sought
> and the more that it replaces the conditioned act of judgment,
> the more that that soul will become free
> and launched into the flight of unconditional love."*

August 21, 2014 (31 minutes)

Unconditional Love

Unfold like a butterfly, launching into the flight of its dreams. That is what all humans are to do—unfold through the heart in order to see the beauty and grace of the Universe, releasing the tightly woven bonds that bind each soul to his own pain. Transformation is to take place, giving rise to the soul and lifting the Light of the world. All humans have come to the Earth for growth and transformation, a development into the soul's lifting Light of God—an energy that encompasses all of the beauty and grace, truth and love that is attainable.

> All are to strive for unconditional love, yet that flight is not an easy one to understand if contemplated by the mind. That flight encompasses an unfolding of the heart, a release of the constraints that humanity and negativity have bound around it. That flight takes place as that being is un-cocooned, discovering its wings and ability to fly. That flight evolves with the evolution of the soul and takes much focus and concentration—a clearing of the energy around in order to release the confinement and misunderstanding that creates disillusionment upon this Earth. One is to strive for unconditional love, as that is what creates paradise—a freeing of the blocked thinking and binding pain and a release into All-Knowing truth, compassion and grace.

With freewill comes the necessity to speak the truth as well as to listen for the inner turmoil that lies below the surface of one's experience. This applies for the treatment of the self as well as for reaching outwardly to encompass the brotherhood of mankind. The more that understanding is sought and the more that it replaces the conditioned act of judgment, the more that that soul will become free and launched into the flight of unconditional love. That journey is a long one—the flight toward unconditional love—and is not to be discredited as unachievable. Yet it is also not to be focused upon so intently that one discredits his own worth for not having yet harnessed that all-worthy goal.

"The key to release is to let go of the baggage that is not necessary—that baggage that was initially carried for soul-development and transformation."

"Once that baggage or lesson is no longer needed, it must be released, allowing the load to be enlightened and the journey to progress at a heightened pace."

The evolution of the soul is being accelerated. Yet due to the heavy energy of the Earth and the negativity that abounds, that process becomes long and delayed by the infringement and infliction of pain that others project forth. It is a cumbersome load to carry—the pains and negativity of another—and until humans learn to release all that they are entrapped into, the journey will be heavily burdened and made weary. The key to release is to let go of the baggage that is not necessary—that baggage that was initially carried for soul-development and transformation. Once that baggage or lesson is no longer needed, it must be released, allowing the load to be enlightened and the journey to progress at a heightened pace.

All of the ghosts of the past must be dispersed and released from harboring continuous pain upon that individual—all guilts, all hurts, all angers, all resentments, all burdens and muddy waters. Those muddy waters of confused or distorted issues, cloud the vision and drown the soul. The goal is to see the world through open eyes with vision that is enabled through a quieted, calm mind and an open, loving heart. When the eyes can clearly see, they will see a world of beauty and Light—one that simply has been clouded over or trapped within the confines of negativity.

> *"It takes understanding & compassion to speak the truth of God & to unravel the mysteries of the Universe to enable eyes to see. That truth must be spoken, & that truth must be acted upon in order to dispel the negativity of the Earth."*

That negativity must be tended to and released from existence, as it suppresses and consumes the unaware. That negativity must be released by the healthy and strong and those guided by the Light and energy of God. It takes understanding and compassion to speak the truth of God and to unravel the mysteries of the Universe to enable eyes to see. That truth must be spoken, and that truth must be acted upon in order to dispel the negativity of the Earth.

> *"...unconditional love does not mean that one is to sit idly by and allow those that harness negativity to spread their pain through acts of aggression and an unruly chain of command."*

> *"The chains that are slung and carelessly whipped about cause scars and unjust rifts of energy that create falsified feelings of entrapment to the victims of that lashing."*

Compassion and unconditional love are needed, yet that unconditional love does not mean that one is to sit idly by and allow those that harness negativity to spread their pain through acts of aggression and an unruly chain of command. The chains that are slung and carelessly whipped about cause scars and unjust rifts of energy that create falsified feelings of entrapment to the victims of that lashing.

One must come to realize that the lashing was requested at some level by each individual victim, yet each is to ultimately rise and shine above that which is unjust. The act occurred to create a quick transformation of the soul in order to release the harboring of insensitivity or judgment or another erroneous act of aggression. Just as that being is a victim of circumstance in the eyes of humanity, he is NOT a victim of circumstance in the development of his soul.

> *"Victims are victims, yet they are not. They chose their fate in order to launch their souls on a quickened path toward self-actualization and ultimately toward unconditional love."*

The perpetrator of that initial unjust act is, too, a victim of circumstance on many levels yet is also experiencing his acts of aggression for the ultimate goal of soul-development. Both the victim and perpetrator have roles to play out, yet development to achieve. They came together to accelerate the growth of each other in a pact at a soul-level. Victims are victims, yet they are not. They chose their fate in order to launch their souls on a quickened path toward self-actualization and ultimately toward unconditional love.

That unconditional love, which is meant to cover the Earth and be harnessed by all, will come to be at an accelerated pace when souls learn to rise and shine and speak the truth—dispelling the negative energy that lurks about ready to smother out the life force of God and silence

His voice. All must learn to live with compassion, yet speak the truth of God in order to silence erroneous pain and judgment that is slung about the Earth—binding and gagging out the truthful beauty and Light that is meant to be.

Freewill reigns, and the humans of the Earth must learn to rise into greatness—not be dragged down to the level of the darkest energy that feeds off the pain and misery of the misinformed. When truth can be freely spoken with compassion and grace and when the Light of reality can shine through the buried burdens of pain, then all will be able to see the paradise that resides upon the Earth that is meant to be spread and gifted to all of humanity through the combined efforts of all.

"Freewill reigns, and the humans of the Earth must learn to rise into greatness— not be dragged down to the level of the darkest energy that feeds off the pain and misery of the misinformed."

> *"Lessons flow into your life for the growth of your being and the transcension of your soul."*

September 9, 2010 (42 minutes)

Life Lessons

Let us delve into the topic of life lessons. Lessons flow into your life for the growth of your being and the transcension of your soul. You must face and confront your lessons head-on in order to unravel the mysteries of your life and soul path. Do not be afraid to look at these truths and weaknesses squarely and with open eyes, for they are necessary for your growth. Hiding from them will only delay your progress and lock you in the past, keeping you from your destined path and self.

> *"When you confront yourself and your hardships with open eyes, you release the fears and burdens that that particular lesson entraps you into—washing away the pains and trials and tribulations of that path."*

Allow the hidden meanings and messages of your lessons to unravel the truths about yourself and the purpose of life. You all have weaknesses to face and road blocks to hurdle over. Denying this and avoiding the truth will simply lock you in stagnation, prolonging the struggles and pains of your current state of affairs. When you confront yourself and your hardships with open eyes, you release the fears and burdens that that particular lesson entraps you into—washing away the pains and trials and tribulations of that path. Through choosing to hasten your progress along

> *"You must settle within yourself, understanding that everything in life serves a purpose for the betterment of your being and the world-at-hand."*

that journey, you will overcome your carried burdens and lift yourself beyond the potential stumbling blocks that line the road ahead.

The road ahead winds and twists in a journey of self-discovery. You must open your eyes and face all that lies in the path at-hand—unraveling the purpose of this path. You must settle within yourself, understanding that everything in life serves a purpose for the betterment of your being and the world-at-hand. The path that you travel is simply that, a path with a beginning and end that branches onto different paths, touching and connecting to the lives of others. The choice is yours, whether to travel with open eyes, guided and directed through God, or to close your eyes and stumble in the dark, encountering road blocks that could have easily been avoided.

> *"The sooner you learn your lessons and face the issues that are being tossed onto your path, the sooner you can avoid the traps and hardships that delay your progress."*

Lessons ensue to teach and guide and to nudge you forth onto the correct, destined journey. Without these lessons there would be no guidance as to which way to turn and what routes to avoid. The sooner you learn your lessons and face the issues that are being tossed onto your path, the sooner you can avoid the traps and hardships that delay your progress.

The road winds and twists, branches and narrows, bringing you closer and closer to the discovery of who you truly are. If you choose to ignore and hide from reality, not clearly defining yourself and the world-at-hand, you will delay your progress into your destined self and soul discovery.

It is up to you to choose your path wisely and unravel this mystery. But it is much easier to do so if you strive to uncover your true self, having the goal of reaching deeper into the truth to more clearly reveal the journey of life.

> *"When you foster a weakness within yourself, you enable that to spread throughout the world affecting not only your being but also the brotherhood of mankind."*

Life is meant to progress each human soul into the discovery of himself, of God, and of humankind. All are connected and all are One. When you foster a weakness within yourself, you enable that to spread throughout the world affecting not only your being but also the brotherhood of mankind. The sooner that each individual takes responsibility for the growth and development of himself, the sooner that the world will be lifted by those individual efforts.

Each soul contributes to the Light of the world. It is up to each individual to shine his Light as brightly as he can, contributing in the way that he is meant to. You all play an important role in the manifestation of paradise on Earth. The quicker that each individual rises into himself and into the

> *"The quicker that each individual rises into himself and into the godly ways of his heritage, the quicker that his life will manifest into ease and unrestraint—bringing to him the riches of the world."*

> *"The more souls that rise and shine, the brighter the Light of the world and the closer to Heaven the Earth will become."*

godly ways of his heritage, the quicker that his life will manifest into ease and unrestraint—bringing to him the riches of the world. The more souls that rise and shine, the brighter the Light of the world and the closer to Heaven the Earth will become.

> *"Lessons repeat themselves until the learning is fostered and the growth instilled."*

> *"All is as it must be, and nothing can be avoided if the lesson is yours to derive. It is better to confront the issue-at-hand with the determination that you will conquer what is holding you back, keeping you from your true self and from being all that God intends you to be."*

Choose your paths wisely and learn your lessons quickly, for if you do not, you simply will travel in circles meandering around until you can clearly see why you are stuck in the muck of despair. Lessons repeat themselves until the learning is fostered and the growth instilled. Hasten your steps toward your soul discovery and find paradise by clearly facing yourself and the lessons that God presents for your growth into your being. All is as it must be, and nothing can be avoided if the lesson is yours to derive. It is better to confront the issue-at-hand with the determination that you will conquer what is holding you back, keeping you from your true self and from being all that God intends you to be.

> *"Let go of your fears of facing truths, for no one is perfect and all are placed upon the Earth for growth and to nurture the brotherhood of mankind."*

Life Lessons

Why sit in the dark when the Light of truth is just around the corner awaiting your discovery? Look with open eyes and unravel the messages and purposes of your hardships. As soon as you clearly see why a lesson appears in your life, then you can take the steps needed to overcome that hurdle, launching you on a new, brighter path. Let go of your fears of facing truths, for no one is perfect and all are placed upon the Earth for growth and to nurture the brotherhood of mankind.

There is endless help in angelic assistance and guidance that abounds if you will only open your eyes to see, and enable yourself to accept the gifts that have been provided to mankind for the purpose of his development. Look to your heart for the answers, and ask for assistance if need be. Help is ever-present and the doors to opportunity shall open as soon as you set foot on the right path, for the road to riches is simply a step away—one that cannot be discovered if you stay stuck in a state of denial and despair. Lift your life to the life of godly delight—a paradise lost but soon to be found—when you discover what you have been granted by God, opening your world to the magnificence that abounds.

"Help is ever-present and the doors to opportunity shall open as soon as you set foot on the right path, for the road to riches is simply a step away—one that cannot be discovered if you stay stuck in a state of denial and despair."

"Herein the problem lies when you live your life trying to get the world to see your reality, rather than trying to see the reality of the world. You must live out of fairness and objectivity—seeking the truth, rather than... seeking the answers that conform to your opinions."

January 7, 2010 (74 minutes)

Mind-Created Realities & Justification

Let us take the related topics of mind-created realities and justification. Man eases the stresses of the mind through justifying erroneous behavior and seeking support for that behavior—yet he does not necessarily seek truth in verification, but rather opinions or circumstances that simply support his own beliefs or ill-founded actions. When you neglect to seek actual truth but instead quest to justifying your own or another party's behavior, mind-created realities set in. There stems a twisting of truth, one created by the mind, in order to justify and convince that a behavior or perspective is acceptable, or even desirable.

This can be detrimental not only to your own inner growth, but also to others who believe in or are inadvertently affected by those mind-created

"When you simply seek to support your own beliefs, rather than to learn and seek understanding and knowledge, you limit your thinking and block out truths."

realities. When you simply seek to support your own beliefs, rather than to learn and seek understanding and knowledge, you limit your thinking and block out truths. You harm others through the spreading of false realities, as these falsehoods become magnified and multiplied when they are relayed as fact rather than mere opinion or thought.

You must refrain from this limited truth-seeking and from spreading unverified information as it hinders your ability to see things as they actually are and from the perspectives of the other parties involved. You limit your world to one that dwells within your own mind and the minds of those that conform to your "story" and the created stories of that group as a whole.

"You must carefully consider the source of all information, and always realize that there are many truths and facets to an event or circumstance."

"...emotion, when not kept in check, can cloud the vision and alter the perception of reality."

Release yourself from your own mind traps, and from the traps that others ensnare you into through their depiction of what they believe to be true. You must carefully consider the source of all information, and always realize that there are many truths and facets to an event or circumstance. Especially refrain from judgment in matters of the heart from which intensified emotion comes into play, for emotion, when not kept in check, can cloud the vision and alter the perception of reality.

"Let go of your preconceived notions and look at life and each event and circumstance with open eyes and an open heart, setting the uncovering of actual truths as goal."

Let go of your preconceived notions and look at life and each event and circumstance with open eyes and an open heart, setting the uncovering of actual truths as goal. Do not simply look for truths that only conform to your opinions—that is "living a lie" and avoiding reality. Doing so does not change the actual reality of a situation, but simply hinders your learning and contributes to the spreading of falsehoods. This is not beneficial to anyone and is not what will lead you to growth and enlightenment.

Always seek to find wisdom and truth—and learning will transpire, burdens will be lifted, and understanding will be fostered. With this, growth can abound and freedom can fly. You will enable others to speak with ease and relax in the knowing that they, too, have a voice that is meant to be heard, for wisdom resides in all. You must open up to learn what others have to offer, rather than to simply force your own point of view.

Power resides not in the avoidance of truth through closing your eyes and hiding from reality, but rather in the opening up to all perspectives and striving for true knowledge. Wisdom lies in seeing and learning, developing and cherishing—not blocking and burdening, hindering and spreading false realities claimed in truth. You are all meant to learn and travel, and to seek and unravel the mysteries of life. How can you venture forth if you choose only to see the world through a limited point of view and not from the varying perspectives and expansive learning and wisdoms of others?

"You are here to share—here to listen as well as to speak. Conversation is a two-way street and clear, forthright communication is goal with the purpose being understanding."

You are here to share—here to listen as well as to speak. Conversation is a two-way street and clear, forthright communication is goal with the purpose being understanding—understanding of a situation, understanding of a person, understanding of a circumstance, understanding of a

Mind-Created Realities & Justification

lesson, and understanding of life. Do not close off to the benefits and joy of conversation and communication by blocking another's right to have his say, and do not falsely alter another's persona by spreading your own limited perceptions as if they were out-right truths. Strive to get at the root of things, rather than to bury another human or perspective in order to lift yourself up so that you appear to be standing on higher ground.

> *"...in most of the world's problems, a simple misunderstanding or miscommunication is at the root. If everyone would take responsibility for his own actions and communicate clearly and truthfully, the problems of the world would be resolved..."*

False truths are unnecessary and often unfounded; therefore, they are an illusion that must be shattered—better yet, not created at all! Take responsibility for yourself and live in reality—the reality of life—NOT the reality that lives in your mind. By keeping an open mind and viewing a situation from multiple perspectives, you will gain knowledge and understanding, compassion and peace of mind, for in most of the world's problems, a simple misunderstanding or miscommunication is at the root. If everyone would take responsibility for his own actions and communicate clearly and truthfully, the problems of the world would be resolved and future problems would be avoided.

Take responsibility to avoid spreading your own false realities. Unlock the truths of a situation by gaining the perspectives of others, and avoid nullifying their feelings, thoughts and wisdoms. Communicate clearly by speaking truths as well as listening with an open mind, and avoid harming or hindering others by passing on your own opinions as fact. Too many reputations are damaged and too many falsehoods are spread due to the inconsideration of others and the avoidance of truth in an effort to make one's self look right.

Herein the problem lies when you live your life trying to get the world to see your reality, rather than trying to see the reality of the world. You must live out of fairness and objectivity—seeking the truth, rather than looking with tunnel vision seeking the answers that conform to your opinions. You will be blind-sided and knocked for a loop if you do not remove your blinders to discover all that you have been missing—all that you have misshaped from your mind's twisting and turning of reality.

"Seek to find the truth so that you can be prepared for reality, for eventually that reality will catch up with you..."

The truth of the matter is "What is, STILL is!"—regardless of how you sugar coat it or how many people you get to agree with you and take your side. Let reality be and do not monkey around with it. Seek to find the truth so that you can be prepared for reality, for eventually that reality will catch up with you—better sooner than later when there is less damage to undo and less humble pie to eat.

"In 'justification' your mind is trying to make right a mistake that you made or a weakness that you have."

Discover the truths for the sake of your self—so that you can learn the lessons that you need to learn and walk your path to joy at a much quicker pace. When you feel the need to justify a situation or to get others to conform to your opinion, that signifies that you have some inner-work to do. In "justification" your mind is trying to make right a mistake that you made or a weakness that you have. Do not waste the time or energy to explain away your behavior—simply look at the behavior, analyze and figure out the issue or weakness, and get it right the next time. Make amends, if need be, and learn your lesson so that you do not find yourself in a similar situation in the future, repeating the same mistake or re-experiencing that particular weakness in your character.

Mind-Created Realities & Justification

> *"All humans have issues they need to work on... Avoiding or justifying these weaknesses blocks your growth and progress, hindering your being and keeping you from joy."*

These situations and their resulting guilts are meant to teach and push you forth along your path of growth. Minimize the growing pains by stretching yourself toward the Light of your being and accepting the weaknesses that you need to overcome. No one is perfect. All humans have issues they need to work on, and the acceptance and recognition of these enable the changed behavior to take place. Avoiding or justifying these weaknesses blocks your growth and progress, hindering your being and keeping you from joy. Accept yourself and recognize the acts of justification and truth-avoidance as signals—signals that are meant to nudge you back on-track, back onto your path of growth.

> *"Accept others and the wisdoms that may spring forth from them, for they are also children of God and may have knowledge that supersedes your own."*

Accept others and the wisdoms that may spring forth from them, for they are also children of God and may have knowledge that supersedes your own. That does not signify a weakness in you, for no one can know everything and no one is an expert in all arenas. But it is a sign of a weakness if you are unable to open up to the knowledge that resides in others, or if you are unable to look at yourself truthfully.

It is a sign of strength to recognize when self-change needs to occur, and an even greater sign of strength to make the necessary changes in order to foster your own growth to positively affect your life and the good of society. Launch yourself into your own growth, for this growth is destined to take place, regardless of your readiness to accept it. Enable it to take place more quickly, less painfully, and with less struggle and guilt by seeking truth and growth, wisdom and Light.

You are all One and all have much to offer each other. Life is not about taking sides and being right. It is about creating understanding and growth and nurturing the life that resides in all. Truth and wisdom create understanding and compassion; and communication spreads this Light and dissolves misunderstanding. Communication exemplifying a high level of integrity, sensitivity and openness spreads the Light of God and nurtures the learning and understanding of all. The higher the level of truth and the more open the communication, the better the result and the greater the achievement toward lifting the Light of the world. Ring truth through your words and sing to the hearts of mankind, for to do anything else is to do a disservice to all and is unjust in the eyes of God.

> *"Life is not about taking sides and being right. It is about creating understanding and growth and nurturing the life that resides in all. Truth and wisdom create understanding and compassion; and communication spreads this Light and dissolves misunderstanding."*

"Each individual comes to the table with different histories, different abilities, different perceptions and different sensitivity levels. These all affect communication style and the interpretation of another individual's words and actions."

February 10, 2010 (68 minutes)

The Underlying Factors of Miscommunication

I shall now address the communication issue that deals with preconceived notions and the misinterpretation of verbal and non-verbal communication. Each individual comes to the table with different histories, different abilities, different perceptions and different sensitivity levels. These all affect communication style and the interpretation of another individual's words and actions. You must refrain from judging another's words based upon your own interpretation, especially in circumstances which are highly emotional or where the verbal communication is incomplete and underlying factors are not visible.

It is extremely difficult to get all the details and facts, hidden meanings and messages behind a situation since humans often avoid in-depth verbal communication for one reason or another—some of which may be lack of time, lack of desire, lack of ability, fear of being misunderstood, fear of being misinterpreted, fear of being disliked, fear of pushing others away, or fear of hurting feelings. Communication is extremely important and is the most crucial and beneficial means of clearing the air—of getting another to understand a situation or of your gaining that understanding for yourself.

> *"In order to truly understand the meaning of a communicated message, you must strive to gain the perspective of the message bearer since the message originates from him."*

To clearly understand another's feelings and intent behind a verbal communication empowers you to better deal with the situation-at-hand and to also avoid misinterpreting thoughts and transferring them on to others. With communication, true understanding is goal. In order to truly understand the meaning of a communicated message, you must strive to gain the perspective of the message bearer since the message originates from him. The source of the message is the speaker, not the listener; therefore, the intended or underlying meaning must come from and be conveyed by the speaker. The speaker must realize this and communicate as clearly as he can, considering the possibility for misinterpretation by his audience.

> *"Due to the vast potential for misinterpretation...there must be a fair exchange of asking and receiving of facts and meanings in order to clearly relay the true message."*

Due to the vast potential for misinterpretation—errors stemming from the numerous factors that play into the way in which one interprets or receives a message—there must be a fair exchange of asking and receiving of facts and meanings in order to clearly relay the true message. Do not be afraid to ask for clarification or to restate your claim, using non-verbal cues to identify whether the other party is on the same wave length. This should occur during the time the actual communication transpires in order to avoid an incorrect or misinterpreted message or meaning from being relayed to a second...or third...or fourth party—spreading and spanning, festering and wounding in an unintentional progression and transference of false information or ill will.

> *"...emotion greatly affects the ability to listen and speak to the intended message with clarity and focus and unclouded judgment."*

Each individual grows through life, receiving stimuli from his environment —from family, friends and society—that shape his feelings, opinions and interpretations in a multitude of arenas. Each individual is born with different traits—different shortcomings and weaknesses, different attributes and strengths. These natural-born traits encompass sensitivity levels and other factors that affect communication style and ability, including both verbal and listening skills. When the natural-born traits are mixed with the environmental stimuli, the combinations become endless, varying in vast degree as to the level of quality and ability to effectively communicate through the giving and receiving of information. Emotion then comes into play, pushing the extremes even further, as emotion greatly affects the ability to listen and speak to the intended message with clarity and focus and unclouded judgment.

When all of these factors are mixed with those of another individual or individuals who have their own communication make-up, then there is even greater room for error in the relaying of a message's true meaning. This is much like the game of "telephone" in which a group sits in a circle and passes along a message by whispering in the ear of the individual next to him until the message makes its way around the circle. Once the relayed message is revealed, it often is quite skewed and translates very differently from its original meaning. This is indicative of how human communication transpires but with many more factors coming into play than the simple verbal and audial ones. There are the added emotional and personality issues, as well as the levels of communication ability and desire to unravel and understand the true meaning of what is being conveyed.

If you feel that you have not clearly received a message, then you must take responsibility and ask for clarification. This will avoid misinterpretation

> *"The difficulty lies in that individuals often do not know that they have misinterpreted a message, resulting in hurt feelings or anger over another's words."*

in both meaning and feeling. If you do not clear the misunderstanding, then take responsibility to avoid further spreading and transferring that misinterpreted message on to other parties. The difficulty lies in that individuals often do not know that they have misinterpreted a message, resulting in hurt feelings or anger over another's words. With this rise in emotion, they then pass the misinterpretation on in order to gain a sympathetic ear and appease their own hurts...or they may simply suffer in silence, feeling that they themselves are misunderstood, not worthy or not liked.

> *"Many relationships are dissolved or avoided due to a simple misunderstood communication, often coming about due to the varying sensitivity levels of the parties involved."*

> *"Body language, tone of voice, and message content can all trigger emotions and alter the perception and interpretation of a message..."*

Many relationships are dissolved or avoided due to a simple misunderstood communication, often coming about due to the varying sensitivity levels of the parties involved. When one communicates a message, he does so from his own point-of-view or perspective, often without consideration as to the other party's interpretation and the resulting feelings that may arise. The message bearer often does not have visible access to how the interpreter feels, his level of sensitivity, his upbringing or his

The Underlying Factors of Miscommunication

point of reference. Body language, tone of voice, and message content can all trigger emotions and alter the perception and interpretation of a message, even though that may not have been the intention of the message bearer. That is why it is crucial for both parties to understand that misinterpretation is a factor, especially with regard to emotional topics or issues. It is necessary to keep the communication lines open in both the giving and receiving of a message in a fair exchange that nurtures true understanding. This, of course, may prolong or extend a conversation, but the benefits must be considered since the main purpose of communication is to foster understanding, conveying forth a particular message and its meaning.

> *"...clear communication...requires the honing of both listening and speaking skills as well as the reining-in of emotion in order to clearly focus on the message and meaning of a conversation."*

Unravel your own truths and clarify your understanding of others through the opening up of your mind and heart. This will enable the avoidance of hurt feelings, the fostering of untruths and the transference of inaccurate information—all accomplished through clear communication. This requires the honing of both listening and speaking skills as well as the reining-in of emotion in order to clearly focus on the message and meaning of a conversation. You must always consider alternative points-of-view and from where the message is coming in both background and emotion, which will help you to decipher the true meaning. The clearest and quickest way to unravel the true intent and meaning of a portrayed message is to simply ask for clarification and do your part to ensure that you are listening well and not making assumptions. When you are the portrayer—the one that is communicating forth—you must consider your audience, avoiding the elimination of material that will lead to misinterpretation or assumption on the listener's part.

> *"Communication is an all-important vehicle for the transference of understanding and the development of mankind. It must be nurtured and perfected through the facing of it rather than the hiding from it out of laziness or fear..."*

Both parties must open up to each other, to the messages that spring forth, and to the crucial factors that lie below the surface—those deeper, anchored roots-of-meaning that must be dug out and unearthed for complete understanding to result. Communication is an all-important vehicle for the transference of understanding and the development of mankind. It must be nurtured and perfected through the facing of it rather than the hiding from it out of laziness or fear that what may be revealed will not meet up with expectation. There are so many underlying factors to what may seem a simple statement, that you must take care not to misinterpret or misconvey a message—whether it be intentional or unintentional—through the misreading or manipulation of nonverbal cues such as tone of voice and facial expression, or through the elimination of crucial facts and information.

> *"The more open and honest the communication, the clearer the understanding and the more effective the learning... launching you ahead on your path to freedom and growth, and enabling you to avoid the pitfalls of skewed information and ill-founded criticism or self-deprecation."*

The more open and honest the communication, the clearer the understanding and the more effective the learning that will transpire—launching you ahead on your path to freedom and growth, and enabling you to avoid the pitfalls of skewed information and ill-founded criticism or

The Underlying Factors of Miscommunication 85

self-deprecation. Launch ahead with determination for the uncovering of truths and understanding, and hone your sensitivity to and awareness of the less-apparent or invisible factors that play in to the underlying meanings of or reasons for a message. This enables the avoidance of unnecessary emotional upsets that may occur within yourself or the other party.

When you tune-in to the individual with whom you are communicating, rather than simply to the verbal message, then understanding is ingrained and heightened and the connection between parties is deepened—fostering a relationship that strives for honesty and integrity while nurturing the true meaning and understanding of the message.

"When you tune-in to the individual with whom you are communicating, rather than simply to the verbal message, then understanding is ingrained and heightened and the connection between parties is deepened..."

"...there is an end-all purpose for struggle and strife. This greater purpose is to learn to create a new and different world... a paradise where there is no war and poverty, strife and doubt."

April 24, 2009 (42 minutes)

Struggle & Strife

As difficult as the experiences and their heart-pained echoes may be, there is an end-all purpose for struggle and strife. This greater purpose is to learn to create a new and different world where there is no pain and deception, no crisis or cause for worry and harm...a world where humans are above all the weakness that exists in the world today...a place of beauty and abundance, joy and love where no fear takes hold of your heart...where love resides in the minds and souls of all that dwell upon Earth...a paradise where there is no war and poverty, strife and doubt.

"Struggle and strife bring about transformation through learning and growth, ingraining changed patterns of behavior and development within the species as a whole."

A lesson of such magnitude is subtly learned but boldly embarked upon at the soul-level, stretching mankind into his own growth and awareness of his purpose and power and the manifestation of creation. Mankind has entrapped himself through his limited beliefs and lack of awareness as to the magnitude and significance of godly creation, hindering his own progress and development. Struggle and strife bring about transformation through learning and growth, ingraining changed patterns of behavior and development within the species as a whole.

> *"All is for a reason, sometimes beyond the visible, that shall lift mankind out of the trap that he has put himself into."*

The time for transformation is now, and is felt within by all of humanity. It is felt at different levels, different magnitudes and in different degrees. Transformation will come to all in each his own time. Honor your unique purpose and timeline. There is a purpose for all growth—and love fills the void in all areas of strife. Do not keep your power locked within, but let it shine without a trickle of doubt, for the glory of God is in all the purpose and all the power of the transformational woes of present-day mankind. All is for a reason, sometimes beyond the visible, that shall lift mankind out of the trap that he has put himself into.

> *"It is your own doubt and lack of understanding for the ways of godly manifestation which cause you to grieve unnecessarily...It is being without doubt that enables you to manifest into a magnitude of Light and love and forthcoming that lifts you into your power-of-being."*

It is your own doubt and lack of understanding for the ways of godly manifestation which cause you to grieve unnecessarily and dwell upon your own woes and those of your friends. It is being without doubt that enables you to manifest into a magnitude of Light and love and forthcoming that lifts you into your power-of-being. Do not be the one to cast doubt upon your own power-of-being, but set forth to lift yourself out of your own trap. Wrap yourself in the love that shines within and hold fast to the dreams that come from deep inside your soul. This power within is yours—yours to keep and treasure, yours to unbury and build into an empire of prosperity and hope, yours to pass on to your children and the generations to come. Go forth and launch a ship of miracles.

> *"The control over your own life is within your own hands—*
> *that 'master of creation' is you, and only you.*
> *Your power is only given away if you choose to do so."*

> *"Mind not only what you think, but also what you feel—*
> *for the feelings are far more powerful than the simple thought."*

An obstacle of seemingly boundless magnitude will have no power—for the power that is, is all within. There is no other power unless it is given away by the grantor. The control over your own life is within your own hands—that "master of creation" is you, and only you. Your power is only given away if you choose to do so.

Power is in emotion, as well as in spirit. This manifests in the physical and is restricted only by the beliefs of the mind. Mind not only what you think, but also what you feel—for the feelings are far more powerful than the simple thought. Feelings are manifested through consistent thought patterns and ingrained beliefs that must be undone and unraveled. Work with your Higher Self and the powers that be—help is ever-present and ever-powerful.

Ask and you shall receive, for that is the gift you all have been given, the gift of your own power-of-being—a being so great that mountains can be moved and oceans can be parted. If you do not ask, then how can you

> *"Ask and you shall receive...*
> *Sometimes things must be stripped away to such a level*
> *where all that remains is to ask and surrender to*
> *the power of God—to trust and to let go,*
> *enabling the gifts to flow and the power to be known."*

receive? Sometimes things must be stripped away to such a level where all that remains is to ask and surrender to the power of God—to trust and to let go, enabling the gifts to flow and the power to be known. This gift, this knowing, becomes realized and empowered through gratitude for being, connecting you to the source of your Provider—the energy of God and His infinite wisdom and power. God is the essence of all.

> *"God is grandiose and the miracle of all miracles. His energy resides within you; and you are able to accomplish as He does."*

God is grandiose and the miracle of all miracles. His energy resides within you; and you are able to accomplish as He does. See this energy, see this Light, and create the world of your dreams—transforming your physicality as well as your spirituality. Nothing is impossible with the assistance of God. Nothing is insurmountable. Nothing is implausible. God is the wonder of all and the grandness of being and creation.

Walk with the angels in the Land of Holy Light—that Light is on Earth as it is in Heaven. A new dawn is rising as the tide rises. God is in the glory of the crests of a fallen wave, in the peace of a mourning dove, in the whispers of a soft rain. The land is plentiful and the bounty is high. Lift your spirit and shine in the Sun's morning light. Open to a new day of wealth and prosperity, peace and love, for tomorrow the Sun will rise and wings will soar.

No gust of wind will fall a bird who has God's wind beneath its wings. Fly high toward the rays of the Sun, into the face of the Almighty, for God shall shelter those who heighten their vision, striving for growth and development, peace and love—launching and lifting society into what is meant to become.

Lift your spirits and soar. Rise above the pull of the Earth's downtrodden and the grasp of the weak and doubtful. Yours is not to bear the suffering

> *"There is no need to choose any suffering,*
> *for that is not the intention...*
> *When you grieve and suffer needlessly, you weigh yourself*
> *down, trapping yourself in a place that is detrimental—*
> *limiting your being and blocking your ability to*
> *help others and take part in lifting the Light of the world."*

of all mankind. Yours is to bear only that which you choose. There is no need to choose any suffering, for that is not the intention. The intent is only to show free choice and free will, and to enable your growth into the Light of being. When you grieve and suffer needlessly, you weigh yourself down, trapping yourself in a place that is detrimental—limiting your being and blocking your ability to help others and take part in lifting the Light of the world.

Be your power. Be your spirit. Be your life. Be your love. Love will heal all and is the answer to all—all questions, all doubt, all fear. There is only love, and love is the only answer. God resides and resounds in the love of all and the love for creation, spreading and lifting the energy and Light of the Earth and mankind away from the pains and drains of suffering and strife.

> *"Be your power. Be your spirit. Be your life. Be your love.*
> *Love will heal all and is the answer to all—*
> *all questions, all doubt, all fear."*

> *"'Actual fear' exists as a signal to alert the body into action in a 'fight or flight' mode of survival...the conditioned thought process of the mind is bypassed, causing physical action triggered through instinct—a heightened sense of awareness connecting you with godly wisdom and direction."*

April 13, 2011 (42 minutes)

Fear & False-Fear

I shall now address the issue of fear, a topic of two distinctions. There is actual fear and there is a false sense of fear created through worry of the mind. "Actual fear" exists as a signal to alert the body into action in a "fight or flight" mode of survival. It is the body's alarm system, signifying that there is negative energy near which places you in harm's way and threatens your well-being or earthly existence. This instinctual signal alerts the body that there is danger present and kicks it into action, at which time the conditioned thought process of the mind is bypassed, causing physical action triggered through instinct—a heightened sense of awareness connecting you with godly wisdom and direction. With this actual fear, the body responds in order to preserve itself, in order to ensure your survival or the survival of another being. God takes the helm and assists through the immediate granting of super-human ability, superseding all modes of typical thought process or action. This miraculous intervention ensures that danger will not come to those who are meant to be protected.

Time, as perceived by the human senses, stands still, and does actually slow down to accommodate the completion of all necessary action ensuring safety for those intended. Time is an illusion and cannot be easily

> *"Time, as perceived by the human senses, stands still, and does actually slow down to accommodate the completion of all necessary action ensuring safety for those intended."*

comprehended by the human mind. In actuality, it is controlled by each individual; and this is most clearly demonstrated during times of trouble when things visibly appear to stand still or flow in slow motion.

God is the driving-force behind these instinctual actions, as the body is directed without connection to the mind's conditioned thought processes of reason. This type of fear is actual and necessary; and this hair-raising condition should not be ignored. The body gives signals even before danger is physically present. If you learn to tune-in and take action accordingly, your life will flow with ease, keeping your own energy clear while also steering clear of external, negative influences.

> *"Instincts are accurate; the mind's dismissal of them can be detrimental. Do not allow your mind to talk you out of an instinctual urge when your body or heart signals an alert to heed warning."*

Pay attention to the body's signals, those nudgings from God, in order to alleviate the potential for danger and to avoid unnecessary hardship and pain. Instincts are accurate; the mind's dismissal of them can be detrimental. Do not allow your mind to talk you out of an instinctual urge when your body or heart signals an alert to heed warning. Train yourself to follow those messages and to notice their callings and directives. You may never know what circumstances of danger you have avoided, but you will eventually come to realize the dangers that could have been bypassed had you simply followed your instincts.

> *"A very different type of conditioned feeling which humans have labeled as fear is, in actuality, 'worry of the mind' ...and must be dissolved in order for you to blossom and grow into who you are meant to become."*

A very different type of conditioned feeling which humans have labeled as fear is, in actuality, "worry of the mind". This is a false sense of fear created by the mind, and it places burden and limitations on your being-of-existence. This false fear results due to a limited sense or misunderstanding of your own power-of-being—your ability to create or control a situation—and must be dissolved in order for you to blossom and grow into who you are meant to become.

Lessons must be learned and limitations removed in order for your soul to prosper and expand, developing beyond the limited constraints of the mind. The dissolving of this condition must take place through discipline and practice, and an opening of the heart in order to receive the true guidance and wisdom that sprouts from God the Almighty, rather than that which stems from the conditioned and restricted human mind.

> *"You must focus on and actually experience your moments of time, living in true reality, in order to escape the fear that resides in an over-pondering and worrisome mind."*

You must focus on and actually experience your moments of time, living in true reality, in order to escape the fear that resides in an over-pondering and worrisome mind. This settles the discontent within, and opens up your world, preventing you from becoming trapped in worry and fret over your own abilities and limited truths. The traps and tricks of the mind can lock you in stagnation, making it more difficult to venture forth toward growth and actualization.

Lost forever is the individual that is so deeply ingrained in despair, that he actually loses himself out of fear of the unknown. This fear represses his being and traps him inside to such a degree that he does not know how to escape the clutches of his own mind's chattering. This extreme is simply a demonstration of the capabilities of the mind's twisting and turning of reality.

> *"All minds alter reality due to the variance of stimuli and interpretation, perspective and sensitivity level; but you must maintain control over your own mind—ensuring that true reality does not escape your grasp."*

> *"The heart, when its guidance is followed, will keep false truths and mind-created fear at bay, while properly alerting you of danger."*

All minds alter reality due to the variance of stimuli and interpretation, perspective and sensitivity level; but you must maintain control over your own mind—ensuring that true reality does not escape your grasp. Humans must strive to seek truth, gaining alternative perspectives and living through the heart in order to properly tune-in to actual fear and avoid the traps of mind-created fear. The mind, when not kept in-check, will hold you back from your true being and self, limiting your world and your life. The heart, when its guidance is followed, will keep false truths and mind-created fear at bay, while properly alerting you of danger. You must learn to discern what is actual fear and what is simply "worry of the mind"—a false sense of limitation that traps and twists reality. This can be achieved by tapping in to the wisdom of the heart—the tuning-in to that still voice inside which is actually a directive of wisdom and guidance from above.

Fear & False-Fear

Both types of fear point to danger. One signals in a warning to avoid danger and the other, in extreme cases, entraps and leads to it. Actual fear is beneficial and life-saving. A false sense of fear is detrimental and life-hampering—crippling the body and life of the individual it leaches onto. In order to avoid the traps of the mind and ensure that true instinct is followed, the heart must be allowed to lead forth. You will avoid the pitfalls of indecision and release the false sense of fear and helplessness when you allow the energy of God to flow through your being by means of the heart.

"Actual fear is beneficial and life-saving. A false sense of fear is detrimental and life-hampering—crippling the body and life of the individual it leaches onto."

> *"Worry is an illusion that must be shattered like the broken glass of a mirror that reflects the pains of life— the misery of all hope gone awry."*

 September 16, 2009 (49 minutes)

Worry of the Mind

Shut out the mind's troublesome pull of mischievous thoughts that bite at your soul's peaceful journey, for peace is what is necessary in order to fully live each moment with joy. Worry is an illusion that must be shattered like the broken glass of a mirror that reflects the pains of life—the misery of all hope gone awry.

> *"Within the tricks of the mind are trapped the hearts of mankind, locking away the true Source of power and connection. Through the heart come truth and guidance— the key to humanity's release. By unchaining the heart, you enable the soul its flight of freedom."*

With worry, you create and magnify problems perceived in the mind. Within the tricks of the mind are trapped the hearts of mankind, locking away the true Source of power and connection. Through the heart come truth and guidance—the key to humanity's release. By unchaining the heart, you enable the soul its flight of freedom.

Focus through your heart and shine the Light of God into your mind's eye, wiping clear the debris that clutters and confuses your soul and

Worry of the Mind

> *"Listen to the whispers of your heart, the messages of peace and love that soothe your soul, for they will quiet your mind leaving it in a peaceful, restful state. The gifts of nature and the Light of the Sun also give rise to comfort and release."*

tears at the very being of your self. Listen to the whispers of your heart, the messages of peace and love that soothe your soul, for they will quiet your mind leaving it in a peaceful, restful state. The gifts of nature and the Light of the Sun also give rise to comfort and release. The experience of nature centers you in "the now", releasing you from the constraints of the mind. The Light of the Sun lifts the energy within, warming the soul and brightening the outlook of the day. Nature provides the visible evidence of God, the reminder that you are never alone and that help is ever-present. That same energy that creates the natural beauty and strength of the Universe resides within and flows through the heart, ready to comfort, lift and guide when you center and tap in to receive.

Seek the wisdom that springs forth from your being and block out the negative, gnawing messages that trap and twist your soul, interrupting and disturbing the path that you are meant to travel. Do not get stuck in a rut, trapped in a time of pain and worry, grief and despair. That serves no purpose, but rather hinders and blocks the Light within. Let go of the pain from the past and the worry that arises again and again from the past path that you walked. You have left that place, and the journey now opens to new opportunity that leaves the past in the past. Let the baggage go, release the worry to God and let the Sun shine in. Let a new day begin!

> *"Past problems were to teach lessons…*
> *seek to learn, finding the wisdom in and the purpose for the experience in order to lift your mind beyond the pains and drains—enabling you to clear your current path."*

You create your own problems, as all Earth dwellers do. Past problems were to teach lessons, but you must move forth along your path if those lessons have been learned. If not, seek to learn, finding the wisdom in and the purpose for the experience in order to lift your mind beyond the pains and drains—enabling you to clear your current path. It is difficult to release and renew, but it is worth the focus and toil, for ahead is a magnificent journey of wonder and Light. Let go of your troubles, trusting in your heart and the healings of God, for He is there always. You must simply believe and let go, allowing the Light of God to shine in—into your soul bringing peace and rest from strife.

"Do not let worry bog you down and dim your Light within ...shine forth and block the mind-speak that whispers the gnawing and nagging recriminating words that can cripple and twist your very being."

Do not let worry bog you down and dim your Light within. You must learn to shine forth and block the mind-speak that whispers the gnawing and nagging recriminating words that can cripple and twist your very being. Set forth down your path with determination and focus on the journey at-hand, not on the one that you have left behind. Realize that that road is worn and has been left in the dust for others to travel, but that segment in your life is over so do not revisit it in your mind—reliving its pains and troubles. Use that journey only to learn and not to hinder your soul and its destiny.

"There is a much greater picture than any one man can see, and it is all within the Divine presence of knowing and support, love and goodness."

Worry of the Mind

Enjoy your life and every step that you take along your wondrous Earthly journey. Look at each day as one of life's little joys, not as a fretful moment used to get to the next segment of your life—that is not meant to be. Simply live and trust that all has its purpose, and all will be taken care of. Live in the peace of knowing that God is at the center of all and is there orchestrating the outcome of events and contemplations of life. There is a much greater picture than any one man can see, and it is all within the Divine presence of knowing and support, love and goodness.

"Do not get caught up in petty worries or small mistakes, but live your life completely in the present and in the knowing that you never walk your path alone."

Do not get caught up in petty worries or small mistakes, but live your life completely in the present and in the knowing that you never walk your path alone. God is simply a whisper away if you will only open up your heart to listen, open up your eyes to see, and tone down your mind to shut out the needless, useless, detrimental chatterings of worry and the past. Let go and let God lift you into the life that you are all meant to live.

Shine forth without hesitation, and untrap your life from the pains of the past and the worry for the future. Shine, shine, shine, my child of God. That is what you are meant to do, not dim your Light—your Light of God. Let that magnificent wisdom of knowing shine forth, spreading over the Earth and touching the souls of mankind. That is your purpose and that is your glory. Worry not and live to live. Unblock your Light, lifting the veil that blocks the Sun from shining in and warming and soothing your soul. Let this Light put you at peace, shutting out the darkness of your troubled mind. All of mankind must learn to do this and shine forth, for through God comes wisdom and Light, knowingness and love, peace and joy. That is what life is meant to be, without the worry and strife of Earthbound life.

> *"...shine forth by shining your Light brightly... without hesitation and through the knowing confidence that God is by your side every step of the way— there to brighten your path when the darkness sets in and there to guide you when your vision is clouded."*

Help the world to shine forth by shining your Light brightly. This is to be done without hesitation and through the knowing confidence that God is by your side every step of the way—there to brighten your path when the darkness sets in and there to guide you when your vision is clouded. Unblock your quest through allowing this Light of God to take root within your very being, bringing Light to your soul and vision to your heart. Heal and soothe your soul through this God-connection, and you will feel peace when you are troubled and love when you are "lost" and alone. Walk forth in this knowledge and shine forth with this brightness. Unburden your mind and lift your heart into the Light of being. Be present always and trust in your purpose and in the outcome that lies ahead.

> *"Take time for enjoyment, as life is not meant to be a burden and a chore but rather a treasure-trove of adventure and discovery, joy and glory."*

Your path winds and moves forth, destined to be discovered as you walk its length. Stop and smell the roses. Take time for enjoyment, as life is not meant to be a burden and a chore but rather a treasure-trove of adventure and discovery, joy and glory. Unravel the mysteries and riches of your journey.

Do not let your mind weigh you down so that you travel in a stupor or fall to the wayside getting trampled by your own ghosts of the past. Pick yourself up and dust yourself off. Open yourself to the beauty that lies right before your eyes—letting the journey begin toward a new discovery of all that life can behold. Live with adventure and wonder and revel at the journey that you create and bring forth by your focus on the joy that life is meant to bring.

Spring forth with life in your step and love in your heart, for you have a purpose and you are on your way. Leave the past behind and launch your dreams of discovery and growth, igniting a world of tremendous abundance and joy. Let peace fill your mind and let the love of God heal your wounds, knowing that He has the power to conquer all. And let the worry be gone!

"Do not let your mind weigh you down so that you travel in a stupor or fall to the wayside getting trampled by your own ghosts of the past."

> *"Guilt must serve simply as a reminder and a vehicle for learning and growth, a checks-and-balance system used to prevent a similar act of weakness from being replicated."*

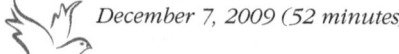 December 7, 2009 (52 minutes)

Guilt & Self-Punishment

Let us now cover the issue of guilt and the resulting self-punishment—both of which are crucial to learning, yet can be self-destructive. You experience the feeling of guilt in order to solidify a soul-lesson or signal the necessity for growth within an area of weakness. It serves as a reminder that this weak area must be kept in check or noted in order to avoid future harm to yourself or another being. This energy that is felt within, serves to enhance your life and push you forth on your path of growth and self-actualization.

You feel guilt and remorse over something from the past that anchors reminders within the brain—prodding and poking at your spirit in a feeling of sorrow or anger directed toward yourself. This guilt feeling often results from a shortcoming or weakness within, that materializes in an action, usually directed toward another. The residual feelings from that experience arise in varying degree and frequency—sometimes often, or sometimes only when triggered by another event or during a highly-emotional state. Depending upon how deeply ingrained the initial experience was, how lasting or severe the resulting consequences were, or how deeply embedded the resulting wounds are, the magnitude and multitude of the guilt ebb and flow.

Guilt is crucial to your soul's growth and development to a degree, but if dwelled upon too deeply it can be self-deprecating and self-destructive—

detrimental to your current life's progress. Guilt must serve simply as a reminder and a vehicle for learning and growth, a checks-and-balance system used to prevent a similar act of weakness from being replicated. Guilt must not be allowed to consume your soul, hindering and blocking out the Light, destroying your moments in time and trapping your life within. That is not the intention and that is not the purpose for guilt.

"It builds sensitivity and compassion within your soul, and opens up learning and appreciation for others and life itself. It points and leads you down a path of discovery which had previously been hidden from unseeing eyes..."

The beneficial purpose for guilt is to point out truths and wisdoms that may have gone unnoticed in the past, and to prevent future repeated mistakes. It builds sensitivity and compassion within your soul, and opens up learning and appreciation for others and life itself. It points and leads you down a path of discovery which had previously been hidden from unseeing eyes—clearing the way for new opportunity and keeping you on the straight and narrow.

"When you get sucked into the hollows of guilt, trapped in the tunnels of your mind, it locks you in a state of torment. This is self-destructive."

When you get sucked into the hollows of guilt, trapped in the tunnels of your mind, it locks you in a state of torment. This is self-destructive. It gnaws away at your soul and whittles away at your self, leading to depression and stagnation. You end up becoming trapped in the past, reliving that moment in time, unable to move on and away from that place of being. You spiral downward in a state of depression, locking yourself within—unable to shine forth and become who you are meant to be. In those moments of self-torment, you get lost in the recesses of your mind and are not truly present for yourself or for anyone else—harming your state of being and your present relationships. This misdirection of guilt must not be allowed to happen. It serves no purpose and is not intended by God. You must forgive yourself and move forward, away from the torment. You must become clear in your thinking and self-judgment.

"Use the guilt as a signal, and carefully analyze yourself to determine if you have truly learned the lesson... If you have, then give yourself permission to move on, be grateful for the lesson, and make amends..."

Use the guilt as a signal, and carefully analyze yourself to determine if you have truly learned the lesson that has been nagging at you. If you have, then give yourself permission to move on, be grateful for the lesson, and make amends to anyone that may have been hurt by your previous actions. Also realize that some hurts scar deeply, and that it may be difficult for another to forgive you for your past inflicted pains. Give them the space they need in order to heal and to enable them to offer their forgiveness. Open the doors to that relationship with heartfelt communication, and avoid slamming them shut and locking yourself away by denying the urge to strike back out of defensiveness.

Sometimes wounds run so deeply that severed relationships result. That is okay—life has its paths, its twists and its turns. Some paths parallel another's, some lead away permanently, and some wind back—connecting

---

"Do not detour off your path in a struggle to recapture a lost-cause—you will only hinder your progress in meeting your destined goals and place in life."

Guilt & Self-Punishment

once again in the distant or not-so-distant future. Do not force the connection. If it is meant to be, it will be. Do not detour off your path in a struggle to recapture a lost-cause—you will only hinder your progress in meeting your destined goals and place in life.

Do what is necessary and right for you in order to reach your destined station in life, following the whisperings of your heart and the callings of your soul. Also realize that others have their own paths which they are destined to follow. All paths are shaped by the experiences and relationships that are encountered along the way. Situations and lessons come about for the growth and development of the parties involved. Look to the wisdoms that result from the situations in life and do not dwell upon the pains—simply utilize them for the guiding lights and path shapers that they are.

"If the guilt signifies a weakness in your being or an uncompleted lesson...then take responsibility to rectify it, seeking the assistance necessary to overcome this hurdle and get past the struggle and pain that dwell there."

If the guilt signifies a weakness in your being or an uncompleted lesson —one that you simply cannot quite grasp a hold of or learn entirely— then take responsibility to rectify it, seeking the assistance necessary to overcome that hurdle and get past the struggle and pain that dwell there. Develop yourself and overcome that weakness through focus, meditation and prayer, communication, professional help, or whatever means serve to transform that aspect into a positive attribute of your ever-evolving self.

"The pangs of guilt are meant to nudge you forth, not to stop you dead in your tracks—weighing you down and burying you in a pile of grief and anguish."

What is of key importance is that soul growth and development are achieved in order to push you along your path. The pangs of guilt are meant to nudge you forth, not to stop you dead in your tracks—weighing you down and burying you in a pile of grief and anguish. No good can come of you or to the world through your lying under a mound of waste, unable to see the Light of day. Push away the dirt, lift yourself up, dust yourself off and allow the Light to shine upon you, and through you. You are meant to shine and move forth to discover your self and your soul's destiny. God's intention is that all humans develop and discover their true essence and shine forth into the world, lifting it to new heights of love and Light-of-being.

"Do not get trapped within the being of your past—
that is not who you are today,
or who you are destined to become tomorrow."

Without growth and discovery, you cannot learn the true meaning of life or find your true being within. Transform yourself and mold yourself to who you want to be. The beauty of life is that it is ever-changing. You are ever-changing. Allow that to be and transform your life into the beauty that you are to become. Do not get trapped within the being of your past—that is not who you are today, or who you are destined to become tomorrow. Learn your lessons and utilize the feelings of guilt for what they are, simply reminders of how to be and how to live—out of truth and justice for all.

"Learn your lessons and utilize the feelings of guilt
for what they are, simply reminders of
how to be and how to live—out of truth and justice for all."

 *February 18, 2010 (57 minutes)*

Anger & Depression

I am here to address the issue of anger and the resulting transgressions of pain. Anger is an emotion that serves to filter the soot out of the mind which gets buried beneath its burdens and the weight of the world. Anger arises when your soul or inner being is weighed down and oppressed for one reason or another. It then needs to be lifted, clearing the energy that gets trapped within.

"Anger often gets pushed down and buried, accumulating after years of self-denial—getting trapped below until it bursts loose revealing its face at often incomprehensible moments."

"The roots of anger intertwine and anchor deeply below the surface, beyond the visible, and must be unraveled and severed in order to release their gnarly holds."

Anger often gets pushed down and buried, accumulating after years of self-denial—getting trapped below until it bursts loose revealing its face at often incomprehensible moments. The roots of anger intertwine and anchor deeply below the surface, beyond the visible, and must be unraveled and severed in order to release their gnarly holds. The feelings and behavior that arise must be analyzed and identified in order to determine the root cause, freeing you from its bonds.

The state of depression is a form of anger in which the anger is directed toward the self in a feeling of insignificance that stems from a lack of awareness of the power-of-being—the realization of your own power to

> *"The state of depression is a form of anger in which the anger is directed toward the self in a feeling of insignificance that stems from a lack of awareness of the power-of-being— the realization of your own power to create."*

> *"When your head is clear and the behavior is top of mind, your actions and feelings most clearly indicate why and from where the eruptive behavior manifests."*

create. Depression locks the self inside in an effort to hide from what it considers an unfair and unjust world and an unworthiness of being.

Often with anger and the rise in emotion, you push others away in an effort to sever the feelings that drag you down and remind you of your inner pain and turmoil. This behavior is often unintended and simmers down once the emotion of anger subsides. It is at this time which you must truly analyze the behavior and note the incident, words or feeling that triggered the reaction and pushed you to your boiling point. When your head is clear and the behavior is top of mind, your actions and feelings most clearly indicate why and from where the eruptive behavior manifests. Recognizing this root cause empowers you and enables you to confront the true, buried issue within that anchors you in pain and thrusts you into moments of attempted release. True lasting release comes from analyzing yourself and discovering the actual cause, cutting the ties that bind and drag you down.

With unchecked anger and unresolved issues you cannot launch ahead into enlightened growth with ease and a lifted spirit. Your Light becomes dimmed and you also dim the Light of those around you who get trapped in your pains. Release is key and effort must be made to achieve peace within so that you are able to shine throughout—Lighting your life and lifting the world around you.

Anger & Depression

> *"The entrapments of anger manifest early in life with conditioned behavior brought about through your environment and un-nurtured needs...With every incident or feeling of lack, a piece of your self is buried beneath pain and fear, trapping and losing itself in the dark..."*

The entrapments of anger manifest early in life with conditioned behavior brought about through your environment and un-nurtured needs. These inadequately-nurtured needs may pertain to your personal inner-growth or they may pertain to the basic level of healthy human development which includes a sense of security, unconditional love and support. With every incident or feeling of lack, a piece of your self is buried beneath pain and fear, trapping and losing itself in the dark—that negative energy that will grip and pull one under. You then attempt to deal with this oppression by ignoring or avoiding the feeling and acknowledgement that particular needs are not being met—burying your self in a loss of self-love. When the weight of this oppression becomes too heavy to contain, it gets unloaded in a burst of anger—much like a boiling volcano that simmers below, letting off steam until it spews forth with hot molten lava.

> *"Once you open your eyes to see what truly exists, and face your past and the situations that trigger your outbursts, you then can launch ahead and release the ties that bind you in stagnation and self-torment."*

You create your own defense mechanism of self-repression in order to hide from and bury pain and to function through day-to-day life—not realizing that if the root issues were faced and confronted, solutions would arise and understandings would be enabled, releasing the self from blame and denial. To face and confront an issue head-on is the only way to unmask it and its resulting uncontrollable behaviors, enabling the true-self to be released and set free from the buried burdens of the past and the undeniable truths that lie below the surface of reality. The answers are all within—within the traps of your self and behind the lids of your closed eyes. Once you open your eyes to see what truly exists, and face your past and the situations that trigger your outbursts, you then can launch ahead and release the ties that bind you in stagnation and self-torment.

Communicate forth with those that you hold responsible for your pain, releasing the tightly woven bonds that grip you. Let go of the past and guilts and traps that anchor you and dissolve your power-of-being. Life is a journey of self-discovery and of revealing what makes you tick. Do not be a ticking bomb waiting to explode, but defuse yourself and extinguish the caustic fire that burns inside.

"You are meant to shine and grow into the Light of love and joy, empowering yourself and those around you. Anger traps that power, locking you inside yourself in a state of turmoil and strife that, when suppressed over time, cannot be contained."

You are meant to shine and grow into the Light of love and joy, empowering yourself and those around you. Anger traps that power, locking you inside yourself in a state of turmoil and strife that, when suppressed over time, cannot be contained. You must unleash your pain and its resulting anger through identifying and diffusing the root cause that entraps your empowerment. With the release of these knots of pain, you will untie yourself and allow your soul to fly free in a knowingness and power that will soar to new heights of growth and development. Allow yourself to fly free in this flight of life, for that is what you are meant to do.

> "All struggle and strife, pain and growth are for a purpose. Once the meaning is unraveled and the mystery solved, the lesson or struggle entraps no more."

> "You hold the power over your own freedom and that lies in the power of the 'now'. The choice is yours to understand and unravel the past, severing the painful ties so that you can live freely today and tomorrow."

If you are unable to directly address the party whom you hold responsible for your pains, then seek to release those ghosts of your past through other means such as counseling, prayer, meditation or contemplation. Although painful, you must face your burdens or fears, as they can only be dispelled through the conscious realization that they can harm no more. All struggle and strife, pain and growth are for a purpose. Once the meaning is unraveled and the mystery solved, the lesson or struggle entraps no more. You hold the power over your own freedom and that lies in the power of the "now". The choice is yours to understand and unravel the past, severing the painful ties so that you can live freely today and tomorrow. Look to all as a learning experience that lifts you to heightened awareness and transformation of your soul. The clearer you see your own path, the quicker you can walk joyously ahead.

Anger is an indicator that there is pain locked within—a signal that there are issues that must be addressed. If you have pent-up anger, the issue

> "If you have pent-up anger, the issue does not lie with the person that your anger is directed toward—he is simply the catalyst...the problem or issue lies within yourself."

does not lie with the person that your anger is directed toward—he is simply the catalyst, the spark that makes you fly into a blaze of heat. The fire is inside of you—the problem or issue lies within yourself. Put out the fire by facing reality and looking to yourself for the answers behind your outbursts. The answers will appear once you examine your emotions and look to see the behaviors or circumstances that locked the caustic behavior within.

"Help yourself and help each other through clear, heartfelt communication which safely and peacefully releases steam and the pressures of your built-up, burdened anger."

In this life, you all have lessons to learn and behaviors and skills to develop. Launch ahead in this development through your confrontation of the demons that lie below, and the releasing of their tightly-fisted grasp upon you. Do not transfer those demons unknowingly and with regret onto another undeserving soul, as each individual has enough of his own demons to stomp out and kick aside. Help yourself and help each other through clear, heartfelt communication which safely and peacefully releases steam and the pressures of your built-up, burdened anger. All anger will be dispelled once you give yourself the time, attention and comfort necessary to address and appease the true feelings that lie within. Ignoring your true needs and what created the feelings of lack, will only fan the flames of pain and resentment until you explode in an uncontainable burning fit of rage.

"All anger will be dispelled once you give yourself the time, attention and comfort necessary to address and appease the true feelings that lie within."

> *"Just as a snake coils to attack, so too do humans when they feel that their egos are being threatened. This twisting of defense tightens their hold on their own beliefs, gripping and grabbing in a struggle to retain the very essence of those beliefs that lock them into the tightly-wound shelters of their minds."*

September 25, 2009 (29 minutes)

The Coiled-Up State of Defensiveness

When man coils up and strikes out at his fellow man, he is torn between his own pains and torments of the mind and cannot see past his own issues and into the hearts of his brothers. He is trapped within his own misconceptions and beliefs that arise from his own soul's discontent—locking him in a state of defensiveness. He suffers from aches of the heart and pains perceived in the mind, which block the Light from shining forth. With understanding and clear, heartfelt communication these blocks can begin to be released. Mankind has blocked his own openness toward his brothers in a perceived state of self-preservation.

> *"All need to release these holds and blocks that they place upon themselves…Only when one stretches forth and surrenders to new ideas and growth can he expand out of his own little world and venture toward new discovery."*

Just as a snake coils to attack, so too do humans when they feel that their egos are being threatened. This twisting of defense tightens their hold on their own beliefs, gripping and grabbing in a struggle to retain the very essence of those beliefs that lock them into the tightly-wound shelters of their minds. Not until uncoiled, can they be free to explore new territory and open their hearts to new discovery—discovery that has always been there but which has not been allowed into their beings as it has been kept out for the sake of perceived self-preservation.

All need to release these holds and blocks that they place upon themselves and open up toward the Light of the Sun—the Light of God. Only when one stretches forth and surrenders to new ideas and growth can he expand out of his own little world and venture toward new discovery.

Your brothers are not your enemies, and there is no need to strike out toward them. In fact, it is detrimental to the survival of your own family—your own species. Through understanding, love and clear communication, wounds—some self-inflicted—can be healed and broken hearts can be mended. Stop judging and harming, but open up to the true essence of each other. Unwrap your coils and open your arms to feel with your hearts and allow yourselves to nurture and treasure the gifts that you all possess.

With struggle and strife come pain, and with pain the Light is blocked. Only through love and understanding can the Light be allowed to enter and shine forth. Often you bury each other in your own burdens and

"Often you bury each other in your own burdens and pains of the past, without the ability to express your true feelings to those who need to hear them in order to expedite healing."

The Coiled-Up State of Defensiveness

pains of the past, without the ability to express your true feelings to those who need to hear them in order to expedite healing. Communication becomes blocked by blocking out the Light of those who try to communicate forth. Release these bonds and let the communication flow freely from your heart without being defensive and without having to be right.

> *"The purpose for communication is to create understanding and to learn so that your soul can evolve and you can be set forth on the path that you are meant to travel."*

The purpose for communication is to create understanding and to learn so that your soul can evolve and you can be set forth on the path that you are meant to travel. Do not get stuck in the traps of your own mind and the self-righteousness of your ego—and do not judge another point-of-view as illegitimate, simply because it may not conform to your current belief systems.

You are all meant to wander and all meant to travel toward your own self-discovery; and you are all meant to heal and learn so that you can lift yourselves up and shine with the true-being of your souls and the Light of God. Do not block each other's Light which only blocks your own. That is not meant to be, and you will simply live in stagnation until you can unblock yourself so that you can, finally, move on.

> *"Do not attack each other for things that you do not understand, from views that have been limited by your coiled-up stance. Untwist your hearts and let the healings begin and the learning continue for all those involved."*

Do not be that coiled-up snake, ready to strike whoever crosses your path. You will not get very far on your own journey if you stay in one place protecting your precious turf and limited beliefs. Venture forth and allow others to present the world to you with new eyes and new ideas—it is all present awaiting your discovery. Do not attack each other for things that you do not understand, from views that have been limited by your coiled-up stance. Untwist your hearts and let the healings begin and the learning continue for all those involved. Do not attack each other but live in harmony accepting each other and nurturing the needs that arise.

To help your brother is to help yourself through conscious living and continual growth. Walk hand-in-hand without pushing aside the needs of each other, and you will all shine in the same Light—healing your own hearts and nurturing your own souls. If you cannot live in harmony, simply move on or stay stuck in your current coiled-up state, but do NOT continue to strike and inflict pain upon others. That is not necessary and is detrimental to the survival of yourself, your brothers and your species as a whole.

There is so much to offer when you truly open up to learn from the unique gifts that can shine forth from each soul of God. Do not block that Light—for you will only block yourself from your own growth and discovery and that which is meant to be.

"There is so much to offer when you truly open up to learn from the unique gifts that can shine forth from each soul of God. Do not block that Light— for you will only block yourself from your own growth and discovery and that which is meant to be."

 *November 15, 2010 (33 minutes)*

Suppression

Mankind must rise and shine into himself and toward the fanciful flight of his being—coming into his own, able to manifest to his very heart's desires. All are to come into this state of existence, yet it takes work and focus, concentration and knowledge—the ability to see beyond the visible and straight into the wisdom of God's shining glory.

Mankind has suppressed himself and the power within—that ability that enables manifestation and the rising of the new dawn. Humanity must kindle a new spirit, one that gives rise to the individual, speaking to the truth and greatness of all in a lifting of society that nurtures the brotherhood of mankind. All must walk a fine line, focusing on good and justness, not suppression and control and the wielding of power over others.

With suppression the life force is knocked out of all, including the suppressor, for to give rise to one's own actual power means embracing the power and goodness of God—as all are One, living and breathing out of God's love and Light, power and wisdom. Suppression serves no one, not even the suppressor, as each individual must be allowed to flow with the energy of God, shining brightly for all to see and revel within that spectacle of being. God's truth and desire is for all to unite, working together in harmony—feeding off the Light and wisdom, strengths and goodness of his fellow brothers.

"When you knock another down & suppress that being, you force the good out of the situation & block the truth & justness from shining forth, masking that life in pain & struggle—suffocating the life force out of the suppressed."

> *"God must then step in & teach lessons, showing the way & directing both the victim & the suppressor in what needs to be shown, shining the Light of truth & justice in a spreading of energy that banishes the negative, harmful suppression."*

When you knock another down and suppress that being, you force the good out of the situation and block the truth and justness from shining forth, masking that life in pain and struggle—suffocating the life force out of the suppressed. God must then step in and teach lessons, showing the way and directing both the victim and the suppressor in what needs to be shown, shining the Light of truth and justice in a spreading of energy that banishes the negative, harmful suppression.

> *"Freedom is a God-granted right and is provided on an equal basis to all races, creeds, sexes and perspectives."*

You must strive to walk toward growth, also allowing others to freely do so, as that is the right of all. Freedom is a God-granted right and is provided on an equal basis to all races, creeds, sexes and perspectives. All have a right to peacefully live their truths and speak their minds without forcefully repressing another being or his alternative perspectives. There is great wisdom in all, and all must be open to sharing and providing in order to strengthen the unity and bond among your species as a whole. Each individual offers a different perspective with different strengths and weaknesses, and the goal of all should be to seek truth in reality and power through God.

> *"God provides the riches of the world, not humans. It is not a human's right to squander what is not rightly his."*

> *"All must strive to live and breathe out of love, with the goal being the achievement of peace on Earth—supporting the equality and brotherhood of all in a giving exchange that balances out the Earth and its inhabitants."*

God provides the riches of the world, not humans. It is not a human's right to squander what is not rightly his. All is meant to be shared and offered to each other in order to serve the brotherhood of mankind and to serve God. With sharing, there will be enough for all—as more is created through the combined efforts of love and truth, justice and Light. Suppression dims that Light and knocks the breath of God out of the situation at hand, blocking the truth and the ability for prosperity and manifestation to result. All must strive to live and breathe out of love, with the goal being the achievement of peace on Earth—supporting the equality and brotherhood of all in a giving exchange that balances out the Earth and its inhabitants.

Through the false representations of truth, lies are spread and the Light is dimmed, harming all that take in this energy either through direct contact or indirectly through the diluted spreading of these lies. This is done on a mass basis through the media and must stop, as it is an unjust wielding of power and a misguided use of authority. It instills unnecessary fear within society, blocking out the Light of those individuals that are meant

> *"Through the false representations of truth, lies are spread & the Light is dimmed, harming all that take in this energy... This is done on a mass basis through the media & must stop, as it is an unjust wielding of power & a misguided use of authority. It instills unnecessary fear within society..."*

> *"Individuals must stand against these untruths, giving no credence to them. This will help block the negativity from spreading...and dissolve away the false sense of power that it presents to the suppressing group."*

to rise and shine and contribute to the world. These falsehoods or exaggerations or twistings of fact are meant to control, throwing more power into the hands of the controlling group.

Each individual must learn to discern the truth for himself, tapping into the callings from within and the guidance directed from God. Individuals must stand against these untruths, giving no credence to them. This will help block the negativity from spreading, allowing the energy of God to take its place and dissolve away the false sense of power that it presents to the suppressing group. God is at the helm, overseeing humanity and nudging forth. His will will be done and the suppression will not be allowed.

> *"You are all meant to live in harmony, living through the only real power that exists—and that is God. God is the overseer and the guider, the lesson maker and the overtaker."*

It's better to learn your lessons while the lessons are more gentle in nature rather than to wait until the problems get out of hand and God must forcefully step in to undo what humans have destroyed. You are all meant to live in harmony, living through the only real power that exists—and that is God. God is the overseer and the guider, the lesson maker and the overtaker. Humans have erred in their attempts to wield their own power over others—that is not their birthright and that shall not be done.

> *"When each individual can claim his own power and truth by living through God, then paradise will appear on Earth. Until then, each godly individual can claim his own piece of paradise through the discovery of what actually is."*

Each loving human soul must take back his own God-given heritage and claim back his own individualized power, recognizing when suppression is taking place. This recognition alone will aide in the dissolving of unjustified fear and repression. When each individual can claim his own power and truth by living through God, then paradise will appear on Earth. Until then, each godly individual can claim his own piece of paradise through the discovery of what actually is.

You cannot truly be suppressed by another individual unless you give your own power away. That is a choice that lies within your own hands. There is unlimited assistance through God which can be called upon at any given moment of time; you simply must ask and be open to receive this assistance.

God grants you the right to live of-God and as God. You simply must develop this ability and awareness in order to harness this energy and spread its beauty, abundance and Light throughout the land—enlightening and transforming your life and the world to come.

> *"You cannot truly be suppressed by another individual unless you give your own power away... There is unlimited assistance through God which can be called upon at any given moment of time..."*

 *November 6, 2009 (52 minutes)*

Relationships

People come and go from your life, creating and forming relationships—all of which serve a purpose to you, or to them, or to each of you. These relationships have been orchestrated through your own doing at a different level of consciousness. They serve to teach and to help you grow—pushing you along your path. All are by choice and, likewise, each relationship can be ended by choice. You maintain control over your destiny, speed of growth, and opportunity for learning.

"When a relationship is detrimental to your well-being and life force, it is your right and responsibility to move on and away from that relationship, or to repair it so that it is no longer ill-functioning and serves a more positive purpose..."

When a relationship is detrimental to your well-being and life force, it is your right and responsibility to move on and away from that relationship, or to repair it so that it is no longer ill-functioning and serves a more positive purpose in both your life and the partnering soul's life. These relationships are meant to foster growth and should be seen as such. They are not meant to harm or damage the soul, but to lift it to a higher level of existence or to strengthen resilience in order to foster independence or Light-of-being.

In a harmonious relationship, the partnering souls serve to nurture and foster growth in a cohesive union. They serve to bond and strengthen the Light and love of self, enabling each to set forth more energy into the world in order to lift the Light of humanity.

Relationships

> *"Everyone is orchestrated into the lives of each other for a purpose—whether that purpose is small or large, there is still a purpose, nevertheless."*

All relationships serve the participant parties in some way—even if the relationship is short-lasting or fleeting. Everyone is orchestrated into the lives of each other for a purpose—whether that purpose is small or large, there is still a purpose, nevertheless. Each partner is to nurture and grow alongside the other, and not to block and get in the way of the other's Light and self-empowerment. That is detrimental to both parties involved and does not foster love and growth.

> *"You must achieve balance in your life in order to maintain the independence of your individual self, while also positively nurturing the relationships that you have..."*

You must each strive to meet and foster your own needs without squelching and stomping on the needs of the other. You are all One and are all brought together for the purpose of growth and love and nurturing. You must achieve balance in your life in order to maintain the independence of your individual self, while also positively nurturing the relationships that you have with partnering souls. This can be difficult to do within the limited time-constraints of Earthly life, due to the pull and pressures that life brings.

You must determine which relationships are valuable and necessary to your individual growth and well-being, as well as determine which relationships bring a positive result to yourself, your partner, the group, or even humanity as a whole. If a relationship does not promote well-being and is not beneficial to the parties involved, it should be dissolved.

Unfortunately, people often stay in relationships simply out of obligation or lack of confidence to move forth, even when that relationship is detrimental to their own well-being. This is not beneficial and is, in fact, harmful to the self and growth of the soul. It prolongs the journey of hardship and pain and hinders the forward progress in moving along the path toward the destined purpose.

"Feel with your heart and tune in to its inner wisdom when making a decision regarding a relationship... choose the relationship's path that leads toward the greater-good of your self and the world at hand."

"Often when one stays in a relationship out of obligation, it not only negatively affects the one making this erroneous choice, but it also damages the well-being and alters the paths of those individuals that are directly or indirectly affected by the choice..."

Feel with your heart and tune in to its inner wisdom when making a decision regarding a relationship. Act from this heart-guidance and choose the relationship's path that leads toward the greater-good of your self and the world at hand. Often when one stays in a relationship out of obligation, it not only negatively affects the one making this erroneous choice, but it also damages the well-being and alters the paths of those individuals that are directly or indirectly affected by the choice—such as those children whose parents remain in a loveless marriage. Yes, It is true that all of the involved parties were in agreement at some level to enter into such a relationship, but the progress of each participant is altered, nevertheless, due to the empowered decision made by those participants in the primary relationship.

Relationships

Through loving relationships—like those experienced by children in households with strong marriages—the paths of the children may be altered in a positive way. They can be set upon their individualized paths at a much quicker pace, bypassing lessons that would have been necessary if they had experienced negative, hurtful childhoods. They get a jump-start on their own destined paths, carrying less baggage from their childhood histories.

"You should not place blame upon those around you for the choices that they make—as you orchestrated these situations and relationships into your life. You can, however, strive...to make sound choices whenever YOU have the opportunity to do so."

Many souls enter into this lifetime, choosing to experience hardship in order to grow and to learn specific lessons. These individuals selected these circumstances and so were born into households and to parents which would provide opportunity for accelerated growth. You all have your paths and your choices and your lessons. You should not place blame upon those around you for the choices that they make—as you orchestrated these situations and relationships into your life. You can, however, strive with determination to make sound choices whenever YOU have the opportunity to do so. You must also look at the role that you play in each relationship that you have, and determine whether it is worth nurturing forth, altering, or dissolving altogether.

"Everything you do and every relationship you have has an echo effect that resonates throughout your life and the world—touching and affecting others that cross your or your partner's path."

Examine your current relationships and do your part to nurture them in such a way that will be most beneficial to your growth as well as the growth of all others involved. You have a responsibility to yourself as well as to your relationships' partners. Everything you do and every relationship you have has an echo effect that resonates throughout your life and the world—touching and affecting others that cross your or your partner's path.

"Be careful with whom you associate, and choose wisely those to whom you open up your life and allow to remain. Your lessons are yours to learn and you learn at your own pace."

Be careful with whom you associate, and choose wisely those to whom you open up your life and allow to remain. Your lessons are yours to learn and you learn at your own pace. Some relationships will nurture and help your progress—allowing you to grow and shine forth; others will knock you down and hold you back—keeping you from being who you came into this world to be. Enable yourself through the people you bring into and keep in your life, and enable those partnering souls by allowing them to shine and by nurturing the beauty of their Light-within. When you lift the Light of another through a positive relationship, your Light is also lifted and you both radiate in a combined harmonious energy—helping to lift the energy of your surroundings and the world.

---

*"Some relationships will nurture and help your progress—
allowing you to grow and shine forth;
others will knock you down and hold you back—
keeping you from being who you came into this world to be."*

♡

"All individuals need be judged only by the quality of their hearts & how they treat other souls of God. They are to be judged by the purity of their intentions & the kindness of their actions, & not by the color of their skin, the physical beauty of their beings, or by any other physical quality with which they have been born—such as homosexuality."

January 9, 2012 (25 minutes)

Homosexuality & Human Prejudice

I shall clarify what it is that God intends to achieve when He creates a child born with homosexual tendencies. That being or soul who chooses to come to this Earth and experience a lifetime of pain and struggle, confrontation and unjust treatment, is a brave soul indeed. He or she comes to experience a life typified by a shunning from society in an attempt to open up minds and hearts, souls and eyes to the unjust and cruel ridicule of those born with differing tendencies from the norm.

It is an effort by God, Himself, to create diversity and strengthen society through the acceptance of this diversity in attempt to advance the human state of existence. God intends equality for all of His children regardless of race, creed, gender or sexual preference. He intends for all to treat each other with respect and acceptance, and overcome the prejudices which have been birthed into man himself through erroneous and unjustified thinking.

Through the Bible there is much translation which can be misinterpreted to suit the reader of the text or the teacher of the message. If prejudice

> *"God is an all-loving, peaceful energy that favors no animosity toward the brotherhood of man & favors no harming of any life, including His children who have come to this Earth to open up eyes, spread truth & soften hearts."*

resides within the writer of the scripture or the translator of that message, then misinterpretation is passed on to society in a twisting of the word of God.

God is an all-loving, peaceful energy that favors no animosity toward the brotherhood of man and favors no harming of any life, including His children who have come to this Earth to open up eyes, spread truth and soften hearts. Humanity should respect all souls who are willing to sacrifice of-themselves in an effort to transcend the thinking of mankind—and those brave souls who endure the painful existence of being trapped within a body that does not measure up to the standard norms of society, are no exception. To be homosexual is not a conscious choice made by that individual; it is an inborn trait just as is heterosexuality.

All individuals need be judged only by the quality of their hearts and how they treat other souls of God. They are to be judged by the purity of their intentions and the kindness of their actions, and not by the color of their skin, the physical beauty of their beings, or by any other physical quality with which they have been born—such as homosexuality. All humans are God's children, and they all come to this Earth with a purpose. That purpose lies in soul development in order to advance humanity and lead to paradise on Earth. Only will paradise be achieved when all can join together as One in order to nurture and assist, rather than tear apart and judge.

To judge one for being born with a physical trait or sexual preference is erroneous. God created the homosexual, just as He created the heterosexual. The intention of that creation was not to hold that atypical being up as an example of how not to be, but rather to create understanding

> *"God created the homosexual, just as He created the heterosexual. The intention of that creation was not to hold that atypical being up as an example of how not to be, but rather to create understanding and develop sensitivity of the soul."*

and develop sensitivity of the soul. Within a homosexual person is a heart and soul just as is in a heterosexual, and man must come to understand that it is not his or her right to judge or admonish what God has created. There has been much twisting of truths and twisting of wisdom in order to serve individuals within humanity and stroke the egos of the misguided.

When this world can open up to diversity and allow others to live in peace, honoring life and nurturing love, then paradise will come. If an individual is living out of love and respecting the life force of others through peace and kindness, then that is all that matters. That is all that is of importance. To judge and ridicule, harm and banish due to the erroneous harboring of a rigid perspective, is unjust in the eyes of God.

> *"When this world can open up to diversity and allow others to live in peace, honoring life and nurturing love, then paradise will come."*

> *"To judge and ridicule, harm and banish due to the erroneous harboring of a rigid perspective, is unjust in the eyes of God."*

> *"The greatest gift that you can grant your children is the confidence to grow into themselves and to shine with who they truly are, not blocking their Light, but watering and feeding their souls so that they sprout and blossom without hesitation or fear into who they are meant to become."*

 August 1, 2009 (47 minutes)

Children & Growth

Children spring forth into this world knowing their purpose upon birth. Soon, with the pull of the Earth, this purpose is forgotten until it emerges once again through trial and error, growth and lessons, pain and progress. Each child must strive and struggle through life until emerging from within is his desire for fulfillment and learning—a calling and a pull from deep within his soul, hidden from the mind's eye until forced into seeing through human eyes. Lost is this purpose until it is brought forth through trials and tribulations that push and pull him onto his true path—usually found once well into adulthood.

Children, young children, are like angels—free and clear in their being, flitting through life on a cloud of contentment—free to fly and free to be,

> *"Children, young children, are like angels—free and clear in their being, flitting through life on a cloud of contentment— free to fly and free to be, unencumbered and carefree. That is how you are meant to live—with joy and purpose..."*

unencumbered and carefree. That is how you are meant to live—with joy and purpose, a purpose of fun. Watch as children play, protected and gleeful. They have not a worry or care that is not comforted and healed with a gentle touch or a simple kiss. They are free to express and are not bogged down by the perceived worries of the world.

Watch in wonder and with awe as a tiny child marvels at the simplest of things. Amazed and excited, he rises with the Sun bringing in a joyous new day. The small child lives life fully with joy and wonder—living as life is meant to be lived. He follows his path and follows his whims unconcerned about the future or the past. He lives for the moment—for that moment in time—not fearing the consequences or possible results of his actions. How marvelous that is! It is what you are all meant to do: follow your soul's inner callings and trust that you will be taken care of.

Listen to the whispers of your heart and let your soul fly free, just as a child lives freely in the moment, joyfully living each day anew. Children have a calling that is heard from the soul. They are drawn toward and listen to the whisperings and pull of this voice inside their mind's eye which speaks to their hearts, gently urging them to follow their dreams and paths that lead toward future opportunity and growth. They are in tune at this special time of life—sometimes more than they ever will be again. This calling resides deep inside, pulling them and compelling them forth.

"Cherish the dreams that lie within a child and the banterings and chatter that come forth. Children are wise beyond their years and know more than meets the eye, for their vision and truth reside within the mind's eye."

Cherish the dreams that lie within a child and the banterings and chatter that come forth. Children are wise beyond their years and know more than meets the eye, for their vision and truth reside within the mind's eye. You must use this as an example and reach within yourself to once again remember the longings of childhood—those that existed long before your mind got cluttered and fogged with another's purpose for your life or another's dream for your future. Within the innocent untainted child's mind is the key to his life's purpose and path—one to be discovered one baby step, then one giant step at a time, until it is so charged with life that he is able to kick it into high gear and plunge ahead into his full purpose and truth.

Wander your way back into the past to discover what you once forgot. Discover what you let others steal away from you or what got buried deep down inside beneath the gunk in your mind. Discover yourself and let the joyous, carefree journey once again begin, a journey no longer lost to your mind's hidden resentments and meanderings. Lift yourself higher into the Light of being—like that of a tiny, whimsical child. Let go and follow your dreams and callings, reining in the fear and helplessness trapped within your conditioned mind.

"You are all meant to live in joy and love, nurturing and peace—growing and developing into your true selves... transforming the Light and energy of the Universe."

Walk hand-in-hand with God as a child walks with a loving parent—protected and nurtured, lifted in the security and knowing of his own power-of-being. You are all meant to live in joy and love, nurturing and peace—growing and developing into your true selves in order to love and lift your own children and humanity into their own power and sense-of-being, transforming the Light and energy of the Universe.

"The road ahead is bright and safe, guided and sheltered, once you set yourself on the right path."

The road ahead is bright and safe, guided and sheltered, once you set yourself on the right path. It is the wandering paths that intermingle with darkness and despair that are not to be followed—for they shall lead nowhere but into darkness and loss of soul. Soul searching or soul seeking is the purpose of life—a journey that is a bright path to follow, leading into a life of childhood play and a game of adventure. Walk hand-in-hand with vision and truth, and let joy lead you down the path of discovery and play.

Cherish the life and joy of your child, watch him grow and allow him to shine. He is a wondrous example to behold. Nurture the life and purpose within and do not block and impede his growth into himself and his inner being. Guide him, but do not impose your will. Protect him, but do not smother him. Walk with him, but do not carry him. Comfort him, but do not coddle him. You are his caretaker, but you are not his keeper. You are his protector, but you are not his weeper. You can watch over him, but you cannot fight his battles. You can teach and guide him, but you cannot learn his lessons for him.

"Today is your moment to take your child into your arms and nurture the soul that is meant to shine and dance. Do not rain on his parade, washing away his truths and muddying the path that stands before him."

Today is your moment to take your child into your arms and nurture the soul that is meant to shine and dance. Do not rain on his parade, washing away his truths and muddying the path that stands before him. Feel with your heart and nurture the needs of the child that you helped to bring forth, as you have your purpose and direction, and he has his. Do not cross his path and stand in his way, but walk along beside him, helping to point the direction, helping to lift him when he falls. Support his decisions with guidance and proper action, but do not hinder the progress he must make in order to reach his soul's purpose, inner beauty and growth.

> *"You hold his tiny heart within your hands. Cherish that being and watch over his growth— nurturing and loving the life within."*

You are his guide and protector while he is in your care. You hold his tiny heart within your hands. Cherish that being and watch over his growth—nurturing and loving the life within. Embrace that child and allow him to be; do not struggle and battle and try to match wits. Assert your loving authority with an open, loving heart, and all will fall into place as you laugh and learn and grow together, walking hand-in-hand down your own paths.

The paths of life wind and connect in a journey of discovery into the self and the world at hand. Walk peacefully and with joy along those paths by treasuring both your own life and that within your child—encouraging growth, diversity and freedom-of-spirit. The greatest gift that you can grant your children is the confidence to grow into themselves and to shine with who they truly are, not blocking their Light, but watering and feeding their souls so that they sprout and blossom without hesitation or fear into who they are meant to become. You are all magnificent, you simply need to blossom in the Light of God without being blocked by the shadow of any human.

> *"Assert your loving authority with an open, loving heart, and all will fall into place as you laugh and learn and grow together, walking hand-in-hand down your own paths."*

"Find a way to fulfill your dreams and get compensated for it—nurturing the spirit and feeding the mind and body, in a literal sense, as the riches and rewards from the toil of your hands will provide the resources that sustain your life."

 December 1, 2009 (60 minutes)

Career Path

There is much to discuss with regard to work—what humans consider to be the toil of the hands or mind in exchange for compensation that provides a means to make a living. You must consider your own personal well-being and satisfaction of the mind, body and spirit when choosing a career, or a simple means to an end.

Feel within your being as to what calls to you, lighting the fire within. What makes your soul sing to the dance of life, lifting your spirit and adding bounce to your step? That is what you should consider when seeking to provide a means to an end. Find a way to fulfill your dreams and get compensated for it—nurturing the spirit and feeding the mind and body, in a literal sense, as the riches and rewards from the toil of your hands will provide the resources that sustain your life.

Let go, and explore what your soul calls to you. Seek to fulfill your innermost desires. Once you do so, you will be led onto the path that will lead straight into your heart's callings, providing all that you seek and all that you dream in a glorious wealth of opportunity. Do not struggle and burden your mind, body, or spirit in an unfulfilling humdrum or stressful job that rips and shreds at your being. Otherwise, you will delay your joy and postpone your life—destroying and burying the opportunities and

> *"You are not to judge your own chosen field of employment, nor to judge another's...All is necessary for the workings of the world as a whole, and all jobs and tasks serve to function and carry out the master plan and cycle of life."*

> *"No one is any more important or special based upon the task at which he toils."*

prosperity that are to live and breathe in those moments of time. Set forth to nurture your being, and the riches will provide and manifest for themselves. There is an opportunity and optimal career choice for everyone. It simply must be sought after and found.

You are not to judge your own chosen field of employment, nor to judge another's. You all have your strengths and weaknesses, goals and dreams, demands and accomplishments to achieve. All is necessary for the workings of the world as a whole, and all jobs and tasks serve to function and carry out the master plan and cycle of life. Seek your special slot in life, and allow others to slot into theirs. It is everyone's divine right to do so, and to achieve complete abundance and joy in life no matter how menial or how intricately advanced a career choice may be. No one is any more important or special based upon the task at which he toils. All that matters is that you fulfill your deepest desires and callings within—those that nudge you toward what you came to this Earth to do.

Some career paths are more simple, providing a life of ease and minimal stress in order to fulfill another mission or focus in life. That is okay and necessary for that soul and for those who benefit from his sharing of his free time. If you choose to forgo a career in order to fulfill another calling, then that is what is right and necessary for your soul's purpose. Allow that to be with ease and knowing that that is what is called forth by God and your soul's inner wisdom.

Career Path

Look clearly and deeply—listening to your heart and the pull of your soul—as to what your true desires and nudgings are telling you. Follow these urges and accomplish all that is necessary in order to fulfill those inner dreams. Without doing so, you will delay your joy and your life, hindering your soul's progress toward its fulfillment of its overall purpose. When this is done, divine intervention takes over, providing opportunity for growth through other means. Lessons come about, and struggles ensue, forcing you to take a deeper look at your life and the path that you have chosen to walk.

> *"Pay no attention to the demands that society or your friends or your family place upon your career choice. They are not the ones living your dream, and they are not the ones that must rise and shine in the day-to-day workings of your life."*

True happiness comes in an expedited manner when you follow the urgings within and launch your life without hesitation toward the pull of your dreams. Launch a career, or lack of one, based upon those callings—bringing about true joy in living. After all, it is your life and your choice, and your responsibility to shape and mold it into that which you desire. Pay no attention to the demands that society or your friends or your family place upon your career choice. They are not the ones living your dream, and they are not the ones that must rise and shine in the day-to-day workings of your life.

> *"If you must work at a task that does not meet up with your dreams, then seek to find the joy and accomplishment that live within that task."*

If you must work at a task that does not meet up with your dreams, then seek to find the joy and accomplishment that live within that task. A simple shift in point-of-view will renew the vitality and opportunity within that segment of your life. See that task as a means to an end, and be thankful for the opportunity it provides in your current state of affairs. All is for a reason, even if that task simply nudges you forth to find something more fulfilling. Dreams are often discovered and launched through the realization that "there must be more to life" than what you may presently be living at the time.

Nurture the opportunities that lie in the task-at-hand. Complete your task to the best of your ability—creating joy in the simplicity of that, and in the knowing that you are doing the best that you can with what you have. That will nurture a pride in you and lift you to a new level of opportunity, simply by drawing forth positive energy and belief in yourself. Touch the lives of others in a positive way through your work and those that it reaches—this, too, will launch a chain of "miracles" in the positive energy that it manifests.

"Work is a necessity of life…
It provides for and nurtures not only the body,
but also the mind and spirit in a social exchange that
brings together the brotherhood of the world."

Work is a necessity of life. If it were not so, nothing would get accomplished and nothing would be provided and available for consumption and use. It provides for and nurtures not only the body, but also the mind and spirit in a social exchange that brings together the brotherhood of the world. When the task is done and accomplished out of joy and love for life, all will be created and blossomed—generating a surplus that creates within itself out of motivation and satisfaction with your self and your life.

> *"Dream your life and live your dream...*
> *All is meant to be glorious and joyful in a society*
> *that creates and balances out, through the goals and*
> *achievements of each contributing soul that*
> *completes the inter-workings and network of the whole."*

Dream your life and live your dream, enjoying your means to create your living through the worth of your self and the launching of your dreams. All is meant to be glorious and joyful in a society that creates and balances out, through the goals and achievements of each contributing soul that completes the inter-workings and network of the whole.

> *"For those of you that choose to stay home and nurture*
> *the lives of your children...This job, when done well,*
> *achieves more than any other job can. It launches*
> *the lives of little souls, enabling them to fly higher and with*
> *greater freedom...transforming the future of society."*

For those of you that choose to stay home and nurture the lives of your children and families, realize that you are a crucial component to the proper and healthy workings of society. You nurture the needs and well-being of others, in what seems a thankless job of drudgery and redoing in an endless responsibility that is constantly undone. This job, when done well, achieves more than any other job can. It launches the lives of little souls, enabling them to fly higher and with greater freedom than if you chose to simply nurture your own needs and seek your own dreams. You enable your children's souls to discover their own dreams at a quicker pace and spread their Light forth into the world, transforming the future of society. You are the launching pad for their lives and the future of the world.

If your choice is to stay at home, do so with joy in order to provide for both yourself and your children—truly nurturing everyone's needs, but you MUST also nurture your own. If you do not, you will not be truly present—unable to give yourself the peace of mind and ability to be all that you can for your family. Your needs are just as important and crucial to the inter-workings of the task-at-hand, which is an all-important, yet a seemingly thankless and payless one. The rewards will be rich and the compensation endless. You will be provided for, if that role is truly what your heart desires and what you are called forth to do.

Nothing is for everyone—the key to joy and the key to abundance is that you follow your dreams and callings from within. Launch your life and fulfill your career desires. Your life will take shape and you will be provided for, whether your career provides the cash flow or whether God does.

"Launch your life and fulfill your career desires. Your life will take shape and you will be provided for, whether your career provides the cash flow or whether God does."

> *"Come to the understanding that pain is a message translating that there is a deeper problem afoot, one that has roots anchored in the soul's discontent. Once that discontent is analyzed and revealed, the healing can begin."*

 *July 26, 2009 (52 minutes)*

Health & Well-Being

Health is a topic that is easily confused with that of well-being. Let go of your preconceived notions of what you consider to be healthy. On Earth, there is a time-space continuum that comes into play that must be understood. You live in a world that rests between vision and reality—what you hold in your mind's eye comes to be. Let go of what you see as reality and come up with a new story—a new vision of how you perceive your world and your health. This, as all else, lies within your own hands resting upon your creation of your own reality through your mind's eye. Once your vision is clear and you come to realize the power that you hold within, your health takes care of itself.

> *"Once your vision is clear and you come to realize the power that you hold within, your health takes care of itself."*

On Earth you have been conditioned to block your own power and knowing. You were born into this world knowing your soul's purpose and knowing your own power, but in time—and within the space of human reality—that all becomes forgotten.

A new-born baby stifles a cry within—lost to a soul bound by time and space and trapped inside an earthly body restricted by the thinking of mankind. He knows no different, and he knows nothing else other than that he shall be taken care of completely. This little child, so innocent and helpless, actually has the world at his fingertips: he cries and his needs are met and nurtured, comforted and honed. He is not a lost little soul but rather one that is treasured and held in the highest regard, loved and sheltered.

Once that child grows and experiences life as it is on Earth, his vision is altered and his needs change. He becomes conditioned to the realities of mankind—those realities that have been created within his mind and passed along from generation to generation. He no longer knows the world of "ask and you shall receive" into which he was born, but instead he finds a world of criticism and lack—one that does not support the one of knowing and creation that he knew upon entering into this lifetime.

> *"Spinning out of control in a cloud of confusion is a whirlwind of dislocated thoughts giving rise to pain and strife within the body itself. All of this is created through the mind and the will of mankind."*

He begins to fill his life with doubt and self-criticism creating a very different world than is meant to be—instead he fosters one that nurtures pains and resentments, traps and stumbling blocks. His will is damaged and his soul is blocked creating dis-ease that stirs within his being. Through this comes falsified limits created in time and space. Spinning out of control in a cloud of confusion is a whirlwind of dislocated thoughts giving rise to pain and strife within the body itself. All of this is created through the mind and the will of mankind.

Let go of the boundaries that bind your mind, stifling your soul and trapping your purpose, for lost is the power over your own thoughts and your

> *"It is with wonder that man cannot see the correlation between his thoughts and his health—the signs are there, the symptoms are apparent."*

> *"Watch for the signs of discontent and alter the feelings or situations that are a cause for concern. Once these are taken care of, the pain will simply disappear and the body's health will come into balance."*

own body's health. It is with wonder that man cannot see the correlation between his thoughts and his health—the signs are there, the symptoms are apparent. They intensify as the stress intensifies and they ebb as the mind and spirit healings begin. Watch for the signs of discontent and alter the feelings or situations that are a cause for concern. Once these are taken care of, the pain will simply disappear and the body's health will come into balance.

Man has given away his power over his own being and own well-being—the freedom that he alone owns. He has placed it in the hands of others and has turned it over to modern medicine and machines. There is so much more dis-ease as man travels farther and farther away from his inner purpose and sense of being. Once the mind is quieted and the soul is set free, man comes back into alignment with his true purpose, relinquishing the need for healing.

> *"Time has trapped man into a state of disbelief... that pulls him from his soul's remembering of the power that lies within. The giving up of this power causes the giving up of control over one's own health and purpose."*

Time has trapped man into a state of disbelief over his own power and control. The pull of the Earth disquiets his mind giving way to havoc that pulls him from his soul's remembering of the power that lies within. The giving up of this power causes the giving up of control over one's own health and purpose. Forever lost are the souls that never regain this understanding of the powers that be.

"Let loose and let God—quiet your troubled mind and the healing will begin. Worry and self-criticism are the biggest threats that tear and rip at the body's defenses, shredding away until pain comes forth."

Let loose and let God—quiet your troubled mind and the healing will begin. Worry and self-criticism are the biggest threats that tear and rip at the body's defenses, shredding away until pain comes forth. Ease the pain and soothe the soul with release and comfort of your heart—knowing that you are a child of God and that you are magnificent and perfect in His eyes. Close your ears to the criticism from others that rip and shred at your ego, for that criticism is coming from someone else who is also "only human" and also has a fragile, damaged ego.

You are all here to learn and all here to help each other, but you all have had damage done unto you. It is your right and your responsibility to take what you have and undo your own damage, yet you are not alone—you have the help of God and His wisdom that comes forth through others. Take this help and this inner knowing that the power of perfect health lies within. Wrap yourself in the arms of God and know that you are His child, given the ability to achieve perfect health.

"Wrap yourself in the arms of God and know that you are His child, given the ability to achieve perfect health."

Come to the understanding that pain is a message translating that there is a deeper problem afoot, one that has roots anchored in the soul's discontent. Once that discontent is analyzed and revealed, the healing can begin. Pay attention to these messages of pain and discomfort for they are signals of a disquieted mind—one that is rooted in agony or misery or loss of true self. Reveal these problems and what will surface is a new beginning, a growth of opportunity that will shake loose and dissolve the pain within; for the shadows of the past, the hauntings of criticism, the constraints of mankind and the blocks of this lifetime will be released and washed away revealing a clean slate and a perfect bill of health.

Man's worst enemy is him, himself, as he has been conditioned to close his eyes to the true beauty and knowing of his soul. Once his eyes are opened he will see the miraculous wonder and marvel that he truly is. Man is a magnificent creature that has blocked his own power and continues to block his own health, creating problems that arise from the discontent within. The discovery of this amazing power will begin to unblock the soul allowing Light to filter, cleanse and heal.

"Man is a magnificent creature that has blocked his own power and continues to block his own health, creating problems that arise from the discontent within. The discovery of this amazing power will begin to unblock the soul allowing Light to filter, cleanse and heal."

This chapter contains two separate but closely related Archangel Gabriel messages. One addresses the visibly obvious "man-created" disasters such as oil spills, economic crisis and war, while the other addresses the seemingly "natural" disasters such as tsunamis and earthquakes.

June 15, 2010 (24 minutes) – Addresses BP Gulf of Mexico oil spill

"Man-Created" Disasters & Negative Energy - Part 1

Trust in the Universe and the vast expanse of its energy. All is happening as it must and all has a solution locked within the wisdom that rests at the hand of God. He is your shepherd and He shall guide His flock to safety and beyond. Trust in His will and in His way, for He has vision that is expansive and all-encompassing, revealing the truths-be-told to humanity.

> *"Man has destroyed much and continues to act destructively with no regard for his environment or for the future of the world...He must learn to think beyond himself and seek higher ground and purpose."*

The disasters that are coming about are for a purpose—one to bring into awareness mankind's vulnerability and the expansive power of the Universe. Man must succumb to the realization that there is a force greater than he and a Master-of-All orchestrating the outcome of events. Man has destroyed much and continues to act destructively with no regard for his environment or for the future of the world. He acts out of greed and disregard, putting others in danger. He must learn to think beyond himself and seek higher ground and purpose. That is why all is destructively

> *"Man...must let go and listen, acting out of truth and justice for all. Once this is achieved all will rest and flow in harmony, banishing the darkness and destruction..."*

breaking down and impacting mankind, in order that he alter his perspective, change his actions and spin a positive Light to keep damaging energy and forces at bay.

Man must stop fighting amongst himself and band together to live in harmony and peace with his brothers and the Earth. He must listen to the whisperings from God that reside within his heart, and release the folly that plays havoc with his mind—pulling him down and trampling his brothers and sisters of the world. He must let go and listen, acting out of truth and justice for all. Once this is achieved all will rest and flow in harmony, banishing the darkness and destruction that reside in the current state of affairs.

> *"The disasters are a must in order to open the eyes of humanity. Otherwise, all would continue to go unnoticed & get forgiven out of complacency & a lack of awareness for the individual power that rests within the hands of each soul..."*

The disasters are a must in order to open the eyes of humanity. Otherwise, all would continue to go unnoticed and get forgiven out of complacency and a lack of awareness for the individual power that rests within the hands of each soul on Earth. All must act out of goodness and kindness, consideration and justness in order to provide what is necessary to sustain human life and prosperity.

All happens as it must and all spurs individuals onto their own path of growth and into their own lessons. Some lessons are mighty big, as is that of the Gulf Coast oil spill with its continuous spewing and spreading onto

> *"Society must plunge into a life that is led out of justice, and banish the greed and competition that surges forth producing negative energy and destruction."*

the coastal territory. This was an eye opener and one meant to change the world's focus on energy and greed—one to launch society into a more nurturing and secure form that takes into consideration public health and safety and the sustainment of the planet.

There have been previous warnings, but due to their limited size, there was limited effect—one that was not long-lasting in memory and one that was not strong and severe enough to bring about transformation. This spill is of such a magnitude and during such a tumultuous economic and war-torn time that citizens must take heed and notice the Earth changes that are resulting. Society must plunge into a life that is led out of justice, and banish the greed and competition that surges forth producing negative energy and destruction.

> *"It is not an individual's right to destroy the Earth or the brotherhood of mankind, and those that choose to do so will face the consequences of their actions."*

If humanity continues to live out of greed, ignoring the signs and signals of destruction, these disasters will continue at an increased magnitude until learning is instilled and transformation takes place. Better to learn these lessons while there is still hope for change, than to be forced off the face of the Earth, never to return again. Each individual must make his own choice: to either live constructively in the way in which God intends out of love and truth, justice and peace, or to not live at all. It is not an individual's right to destroy the Earth or the brotherhood of mankind, and those that choose to do so will face the consequences of their actions.

> *"It is up to humanity to hold strong and ensure that human rights prevail and unjust behavior is duly punished in order to stop the destructive force that the power-hungry wield."*

Individuals must take a stand in order to banish this negativity from the Earth. Each must rise and shine into his own power, speaking his own mind and the truth of God in order to give voice to just-cause and help save the brotherhood of mankind. It is up to humanity to hold strong and ensure that human rights prevail and unjust behavior is duly punished in order to stop the destructive force that the power-hungry wield.

The disasters signify an uprising of the negative energy that spews forth, and it is within the power of mankind to put this to rest and appease the souls of the world and God Himself. No longer harbor negativity and resentment, but work together toward peace—enlightening the souls of mankind and lifting the energy of the world in order to alleviate the effects of disasters and to prevent them all together.

> *"No longer harbor negativity and resentment, but work together toward peace— enlightening the souls of mankind and lifting the energy of the world in order to alleviate the effects of disasters and to prevent them all together."*

> *"...unrest among the population of the Earth...
> is of such heightened intensity that it is bringing about
> disaster in a grand magnitude of upheaval."*

March 11, 2011 (26 minutes) – Addresses Japan's tsunami & earthquakes

"Natural" Disasters & Negative Energy - Part 2

The matter of the tsunami, earthquakes and various other "natural" disasters signals an unrest among the population of the Earth. The negative energy is of such heightened intensity that it is bringing about disaster in a grand magnitude of upheaval. The people of the world must pull together to support and aid, rather than to ravish and rip at each other's doorsteps, bringing down the empires of the world. Those empires are needed to aid and assist with purity and strength in order to alleviate the negative energies that spiral out of control, causing the tumultuous results that leave shadows of death and destruction.

> *"You each must act on your own accord, calling forth
> through prayer the powers-that-be
> in loving protection and a bringing of peace."*

You each must act on your own accord, calling forth through prayer the powers-that-be in loving protection and a bringing of peace. There are souls banding together throughout the world in order to lift this energy and help bring about peace for the entirety of mankind. Rest assured that

> *"the barriers of protection...must be rebuilt in a stronger, more forceful way...consciously built upon the time-honored principles of love and truth, justice and God."*

God will prevail, sheltering His children—those that strive to live out of goodness and love. All others will suffer the consequences of their destructive demeanors and closed-off hearts.

The hearts of the new world need to be free and clear of self-importance and unnecessary judgment and anger toward others. These have brought down the barriers of protection that had previously resulted out of love for one another and God Himself. These barriers have been eroded over time and must be rebuilt in a stronger, more forceful way—one which will withstand the test of time—a stronghold consciously built upon the time-honored principles of love and truth, justice and God.

> *"It is not God that has brought about these disasters— it is man and those unworthy sources of negativity that some individuals have called upon in order to create a sense of power and control to hoard and hold over others."*

The disasters simply show man how insignificant his strength and power are, bringing him down to his knees in an act of surrender to the powers-that-be. They demonstrate to him that he must turn to God for support and guidance rather than take matters into his own hands. Those matters have resulted in an unjust wielding of power, bringing about strife and pain, destruction and death. Man is his own worst enemy, bringing about much more than he even fathoms. It is not God that has brought about these disasters—it is man and those unworthy sources of negativity that some individuals have called upon in order to create a sense of power and control to hoard and hold over others.

When man understands the true importance of life, love and freely giving of himself, then the world will settle into itself—bringing about peace and calm in a cohesion of unity that frees all. The Earth will then balance out and repair itself, relaxing into its own spirit and energy of peace.

> *"Man...continues to reap the natural resources of the Earth while sowing seeds of hate and denial— not taking responsibility for his own actions but falsely blaming others for what he has destroyed."*

> *"Until man understands what he is doing, he will simply punish himself through the harboring and reallocating of this same negative energy that he spews forth."*

Man does not understand the energy he emits through his thoughts and countless acts of aggression. He does not understand the degree of destruction that he harbors within his very hands. He continues to reap the natural resources of the Earth while sowing seeds of hate and denial—not taking responsibility for his own actions but falsely blaming others for what he has destroyed. Until man understands what he is doing, he will simply punish himself through the harboring and reallocating of this same negative energy that he spews forth.

Do not fret over the disasters that are occurring and those that are on the horizon—if you are meant to be protected then you will be. Simply have faith and trust in the powers-that-be, settle within your heart, keep your energy clear without harboring negativity, and pray and ask for guidance. Play out your role constructively, lifting the Light of those around you and positively affecting the world in a peaceful exchange of truth and justice.

Disasters & Negative Energy

Rid yourself from dwelling upon the negativity and despair that are necessary to teach such bold lessons to those that are too blind to see—those that simply turn their heads and state "not to sweat the small stuff". Unfortunately, those blind eyes will eventually be opened when that "small stuff" knocks them upside the head or wipes them off their feet. If knocked too hard, they may be wiped clean off the Earth, never to return again.

The time for change is now, and humanity better make that change quickly, for the dawn is rising and not all will awaken to rise and shine in the times to come. The Earth is weeding out the negativity so that a new peaceful existence can come to be, sprouting a paradise that shall rise and shine in the Light of God. Walk hand-in-hand with God and each other, supporting and transcending the Light of the world, and you shall walk with grace into a land of peace and beauty, love and holy Light.

"The Earth is weeding out the negativity so that a new peaceful existence can come to be, sprouting a paradise that shall rise and shine in the Light of God."

> *"In death the body is laid to rest in a quiet eternal sleep
> and returns to the earth from which it sprang.
> At the point of the soul's ascent, it flies free to whence
> it came—back into the outstretched arms of God..."*

February 3, 2010 (71 minutes)

Death of the Body – Ascent of the Soul

In death the body is laid to rest in a quiet eternal sleep and returns to the earth from which it sprang. At the point of the soul's ascent, it flies free to whence it came—back into the outstretched arms of God, back home to its Creator, the magnificent and almighty Master of all creation and center of the Universe. During this flight of freedom the soul is released from its Earthly bonds and relaxes into the ease and unrestraint of all-knowing truth, wisdom and Light. It is lifted away from the drains and pull of Earthly woes, struggle and strife. It settles into the freedom of truths that expand beyond the human mind in an ever-presence of complete knowledge, Light and healing essence—releasing the traps and constraints of life. The soul finds its way home once it releases its bond to life and severs the connections that anchor it to its Earthly ties.

> *"For some tormented souls that dwell in
> unfinished business, the flight to freedom is delayed
> until that soul completes its lessons,
> allowing it to then move forth and fly toward the Light."*

Death of the Body – Ascent of the Soul

For some tormented souls that dwell in unfinished business, the flight to freedom is delayed until that soul completes its lessons, allowing it to then move forth and fly toward the Light. These souls are ones that were lost during their Earthly life, trapped in a life of torment and pain rooted in lessons of major growth and individualized transformation. With this unfinished business that did not get settled during the Earthly life, the soul must continue forth in order to complete the process at a different level of existence until the lesson or soul growth is satisfactorily achieved. The degree of soul growth that transpires determines the destiny of that soul and to where it must then fly—back into another life of continued pain and advanced soul growth, or on to another means of transformation through a more satisfying lifetime or spiritual experience.

"For those souls that led an enlightened and more complete life…the soul flies free into the loving arms of God and the outstretched connected Light of other souls that encompass its same energy and Light."

For those souls that led an enlightened and more complete life—one in which they nurtured others and spread the Light of love and truth, justice and kindness—the soul flies free into the loving arms of God and the outstretched connected Light of other souls that encompass its same energy and Light. This family of souls band together in a radiant energy that lifts the Light of its still-anchored Earthbound members, nudging and guiding, comforting and directing when need be. The souls remain connected in some form, either in an angelic state-of-presence or in a reincarnation of that energy into another being whose life will interweave with that group or family of embodied souls. It is to be noted that members of a soul family are often not members of one's human family, and vice versa.

You are always connected with your soul family to some degree—growing and prospering, learning and lifting—in a progression of heightened evolution and lifted Light that transforms the entire soul family for the generations to come, contributing to the transcendence of mankind. Growth and enlightenment can be quickened for the entire group with the expansion of an individual soul during an Earthly lifetime or through the development and transcendence of that soul while on a different plane of existence. The souls of the soul family are woven together and connected by threads of Light anchored through God's energy. Growth and, thus, transformation is the goal in order to lift that family and, eventually, the entire race of humanity to a heightened level of being.

"During the Earthly lifetime of a soul, it can at any given time tap into the energy & wisdom of its soul family or to that of God...Prayer is the vehicle for the asking & the heart is the vehicle for the receiving in a giftful exchange of Light & love & the interconnection of God..."

During the Earthly lifetime of a soul, it can at any given time tap into the energy and wisdom of its soul family or to that of God. This is done through the heart and through feeling with focus. Prayer is the vehicle for the asking and the heart is the vehicle for the receiving in a giftful exchange of Light and love and the interconnection of God, His wisdom and energy.

"Once the soul discovers its purpose & also its source of creation & freedom—which is God and its own power to create—it is released from the burdens of struggle & strife."

"The soul's journey on Earth is...to learn how to fly... to spread its wings, trust, & lift its own Earthly life to the level that it was meant to reach, the level of godly creation..."

Death of the Body – Ascent of the Soul

The soul is meant to fly free, even during its waking life on Earth. It is meant to fly toward the discovery of its own beauty and Light and reach beyond the limited constraints of its Earthly body and burdened mind. Once the soul discovers its purpose and also its source of creation and freedom—which is God and its own power to create—it is released from the burdens of struggle and strife. The soul's journey on Earth is to discover this beauty and to learn how to fly—not fly out of its Earthly body as it does upon death—but to learn how to spread its wings, trust, and lift its own Earthly life to the level that it was meant to reach, the level of godly creation and manifestation.

The soul's journey through Earthbound life is one of discovery and growth, bringing it closer and closer to the seeing and realization of its own beauty as reflected in the eyes of God. Man must learn to see this and experience his own individualized gifts in order to shape his path into a joyous journey of creation—transforming his current life's destiny, his future lives, his soul group's transformation in its current state as well as in future generations to come, and the destiny of humanity as a whole. Each soul plays an integral part in the lifting of lives and the sharing of growth and enlightenment.

"Upon death the soul is released & given reprieve... allowing it complete freedom & flight, knowingness & Light. During this state the soul is able to prepare & decide upon its next journey of transformation & soul development..."

Upon death the soul is released and given reprieve from the hard and draining Earthly life, allowing it complete freedom and flight, knowingness and Light. During this state the soul is able to prepare and decide upon its next journey of transformation and soul development in order to help shape the world-to-come and its destiny for creation. This reprieve is necessary in order to prepare for the upcoming journey.

> *"Humans are not perfect and their path is one of learning and growth. Good intention is key and selfless giving is goal."*

Death is not to be feared for those that strive to live a good, kind life of growth and progress. Humans are not perfect and their path is one of learning and growth. Good intention is key and selfless giving is goal. Mistakes are inevitable, that is what spurs the desire to learn and transform your being—your soul. Progress ensues from the desire to mend, allowing growth to settle in and launch transformation. When you look to God for the answers and strive to live in the Light of His wisdom, you can do no wrong, for the intention to aid your brothers is there and that is the key to humanity's growth—to shine in the Light of God, knowing that you all come from the same source of Light and creation.

> *"The souls that struggle upon death,
> do have something to fear in that there is a prolonged
> stagnation of the soul which locks them in torment...
> This is caused by a loss of self, a disconnection
> from the source of God during that soul's Earthly lifetime...
> created from a turning away from the Light
> and a shunning of the brotherhood of mankind."*

The souls that struggle upon death, do have something to fear in that there is a prolonged stagnation of the soul which locks them in torment—a state of limbo in which they do not know where to turn or where to go. This is caused by a loss of self, a disconnection from the source of God during that soul's Earthly lifetime. It is created from a turning away from the Light and a shunning of the brotherhood of mankind. When this is done, that soul must remain in a state of stagnation and experience soul-growth in a state of unrest. Transformation must take place to

> *"All life paths are established before birth, yet free will remains and lessons can be quickened or bypassed based upon that soul's desire for and seeking of growth, and through the realization that it creates its own reality and brings about its own lessons for transformation."*

> *"...all life is meant to be treasured & nurtured, loved & honored."*

some degree during this state in order for that soul to no longer repeat the same harmful, relentless, detrimental mistakes of the past lifetime. Lessons must be learned in order for that soul to be allowed to move on and away from its state of discontent.

All life paths are established before birth, yet free will remains and lessons can be quickened or bypassed based upon that soul's desire for and seeking of growth, and through the realization that it creates its own reality and brings about its own lessons for transformation. All are meant to uncover and unravel the mysteries of life and to center in the conclusion that all life is meant to be treasured and nurtured, loved and honored. With this realization man will lift himself into a heightened level of being and will bypass the lessons that bring about pain, struggle and strife. The sooner that man comes to realize the powers-that-be and the purpose for life, the sooner he can transform his own life and contribute to the lifting of mankind as a whole, bringing about the glory and paradise on Earth that is meant to be.

Each soul has its destined purpose, yet all are meant to lead to the guidance and lifting of life and humanity. The sooner you realize your own

> *"Each soul has its destined purpose, yet all are meant to lead to the guidance and lifting of life and humanity."*

individualized purpose, power, and effect upon the greater picture of life, the sooner you can spread your Light with focus and clarity.

Death is simply a reprieve from life utilized to shape and plan your future lives-to-come—connecting you back to your Source and soul family and, once again, lift the Light of your soul in a pure freedom that is not easily enabled during your Earthly life. God is always present—during your Earthly life, upon your Earthly death, and after your soul's ascent. He is always there to call upon, ready to aid when asked, and is always nudging and giving guidance—if you will only tune in to listen through your heart and with your soul. He is there for every soul's assistance, those that freely fly toward the Light and those that are trapped and lost in the dark.

Lift your faith, as God is all and God will prevail. Where there is a will, there is always a way—a way into the Light, even from the darkest deepest depths. You simply need to ask and you need to listen, you need to follow and you need to allow the Light to shine—lifting you back to your Source of creation, power, love and lightness-of-being. God is ever-present and the Source of all good—dispelling all negativity and sorrow, lack and fear. Simply tune in and live your life knowing that you are a child of God and are meant to shine in His Light and live His dream with the energy and intention of good and Light, love and creation. Then all will be well and peaceful during your Earthbound life and in the hereafter.

"Lift your faith, as God is all and God will prevail.
Where there is a will, there is always a way—
a way into the Light, even from the darkest deepest depths.
You simply need to ask and you need to listen,
you need to follow and you need to allow the Light to shine..."

♡

Section III
Individual Purpose & Self-Discovery

The world is your oyster. You are the pearl.

Over the sands of time the waters of the Earth wash—

building and buffing, shaping and smoothing,

creating a deeply ingrained sheen and layered beauty...

a treasure to behold.

Lift your eyes to the sky to experience the wonder of it all—all joy, all release, all glory and all peace. The world is your oyster and you are the pearl. It is high time that you throw off that shell and let your colors dance in the Light to brighten the surrounding world. You are to let the breath of God lift your spirit and shine beauty and Light upon the darkness that has been previously experienced. This glory is within your hands, yours to shape and mold and launch into a magical world of existence that is meant to flourish in the beauty of "you" combined with God's resources. Now is the time to shine to brighten your world within and throughout the surrounding atmosphere.

> *"You are all meant to shine and not to cast dark shadows, blocking the Light of those around you."*

 *July 27, 2009 (22 minutes)*

Shine Your Light

You are all prisms of Light. Keep your energy clear and your mind and judgment unclouded. Bring the Light of God into your being reflecting and refracting His presence and your true selves within, Lighting the world around you—gloriously changing the colors and beauty of the Universe. You are all meant to shine and not to cast dark shadows, blocking the Light of those around you. You each have your own gifts and purpose, spreading a Light of different colors and patterns for all to see and revel in—creating a kaleidoscope of magnificent rainbow hues that interplay with the golden-rich rays of godly delight.

Watch and marvel in the glory of the Kingdom to come, for you all have your roles to play and your Light to shine. You all play a part in this tapestry-woven world, adding sparkle when your fire is lit within by the flame of God's presence. Oh, what glory this world can become when the Light of each conscious soul is ignited and allowed to burn. Give oxygen to your purpose and let God breathe life-force into your soul—for no other moment cascades so perfectly and burns so deeply.

> *"Let your mind and soul fly free, untrapping your purpose within. Allow yourself to shine and burn brightly with the rich hues that are yours, and yours alone."*

I am the eye of God, the one that watches over you, protecting and giving hope when there is despair. Let your mind and soul fly free, untrapping your purpose within. Allow yourself to shine and burn brightly with the rich hues that are yours, and yours alone. See your gifts as God sees them and allow them to shine from within. Do not let others throw a blanket of darkness upon you—smothering that flame and that life until it smolders out like a candle that has been snuffed. You are meant to shine and to do so brightly. Glow strong and with brilliance, for that is your purpose, that is your gift, that is your Light, and that is your right.

You are all multidimensional and multifaceted, reflecting the Light—your Light and the Light of God—in different ways. Your rays bounce and play off the rays of each other, dancing to the music of life, creating a Light show of magic in the Kingdom of tomorrow and today—for that magic is present now, if you will only open your eyes to see.

You live in a world filled with the creation of the Universe and the magic of God's souls; you simply need to encompass the energy of God to open up your eyes and remove the veil of fog that lids your vision and masks your being. All is ever-present in a sparkling world that has no bounds or limits—one that is only hindered by the limited thinking of man himself. No longer halt your soul's progress and that of mankind as a whole, for what is the purpose in that? All that results is struggle and strife and sorrow and guilt—all unnecessary and not intended by God. God's true choice is for man to fully become into being, lifting his soul to shine throughout the Kingdom in heavenly glory. Shine your significance and Light, contributing to the development and magnificence of the world.

"All is ever-present in a sparkling world that has no bounds or limits—one that is only hindered by the limited thinking of man himself."

> *"You must take charge of your own life. Take control of your emotions and realize your own worth...the worth that has been bestowed upon you by God the Almighty..."*

 *July 4, 2009 (45 minutes)*

Life is a Journey!

You must take charge of your own life. Take control of your emotions and realize your own worth—not the worth that has been placed upon you by your parents or those that you have met along your travels, but the worth that has been bestowed upon you by God the Almighty—the one with the wisdom and true knowing, the seeker of beauty and individuality, the commander of all love and glory, joy and life.

Thrust forward into life and do not look back with regret or longing for what "should have been" or for what was "meant to be". The path that you have walked has had its purpose as all paths do, but it was just a path—one left in the dust, one left to be erased and eroded over time. Time heals all but can be quickened, as your steps can also be quickened. You can leap forward into life or you can simply lie down and die. It is your choice for the choosing and your choice to take action upon.

Look ahead and not behind, for what good does it do to look back? It only slows down the progress of life and growth, and revisits that which

> *"Why live in the past when there is so much more to create? Life is limitless unless you place limits upon your life."*

no longer needs to be seen or dwelled upon. Why live in the past when there is so much more to create? Life is limitless unless you place limits upon your life. It is yours for the asking, yours for the seeking, yours for the believing and yours for the taking. Ask and you shall receive. That is your birthright and that is your gift.

> *"You have your gifts and they are unique to you. You must allow them to shine and to touch the world without reservation and without worry or shame."*

> *"Choose your path and choose the direction in which you turn—away from the Light or toward the bright sunshine and days of glory."*

You have your gifts and they are unique to you. You must allow them to shine and to touch the world without reservation and without worry or shame. Shame is placed upon those in need at a young age and must be worked upon in order to overcome the falsities and burdens that it places upon lives. It is part of life's journey, at least for that life. That path, when walked, has brush that must be cleared. There is purpose which will be seen when the Light shines through the thicket as the dawn brings the Sun. The Sun will rise and shine, lifting the heads of those that look toward the Light, turning away the heads of those that choose not to see. Choose your path and choose the direction in which you turn—away from the Light or toward the bright sunshine and days of glory.

> *"Growth brings pain but also wonder and success, courage and compassion, understanding and will."*

"Feel with your heart and you will be led...for in the mind dwell the questions, but in the heart live the answers."

All that is "meant to be" is, and all has its purpose. Growth brings pain but also wonder and success, courage and compassion, understanding and will. Feel with your heart and you will be led to all the answers that question your troubled mind, for in the mind dwell the questions, but in the heart live the answers. The heart is the tuning fork of God, the receiver for human emotion and understanding. All the answers are found where the heart meets Light—the middle place, the power center of the soul, the meeting of the Universe and the human spirit. Allow the soul to take flight and nothing can stop its ascent, an ascent into higher understanding and an awareness of the power that connects it to the Almighty God. Life is limitless when this union is found and understood.

"There is no boundary that can be drawn or that can separate the Source from its children. That is a connection that cannot be broken unless that individual severs its own ties, its own umbilical cord to the life-force which created it."

There is no boundary that can be drawn or that can separate the Source from its children. That is a connection that cannot be broken unless that individual severs its own ties, its own umbilical cord to the life-force which created it. You are all meant to journey—to journey to discover this incredible, limitless connection. The sooner the connection is made, the sooner the path will brighten and open to a paradise lost behind a masquerade of thicket and brush. Once that brush is cleared, once the demons are confronted, you will see that the only blocks were ones that existed in your mind, created from false beliefs rooted in your past. Look only ahead and create the life that you wish to live, for in beauty and joy there is life, not stumbling blocks that play havoc with your ego.

*"You are all meant to journey—
to journey to discover this incredible, limitless connection.
The sooner the connection is made, the sooner...you will see
that the only blocks were ones that existed
in your mind, created from false beliefs rooted in your past."*

*"Enjoy every moment in time, realizing and experiencing
the incredible journey that you are on..."*

Enjoy every moment in time, realizing and experiencing the incredible journey that you are on and the incredible journey that awaits you. Life is meant to be lived with ease and adventure, not roadblocks and stockades. Kick over those detour signs and focus only upon what lies ahead, not upon what you have run over during your bumpy ride. Give your engine some gas and do not let it run dry—do not get stuck in a place where you do not want to be. Prepare for the ride of your life, take the wheel and hold on, for an adventure awaits when you are ready to roll. Move forward with ease, expect the unexpected and there will be no surprises that knock you off the road.

God is there to protect you from a fall or to buffer the guardrail if need be. Your path is your destiny and you are never alone. You may not see those that watch over you, but you are watched over every moment of every day. Nothing can harm you, nothing can shake the ground or quake the earth unless you have agreed

*"Your path is your destiny and you are never alone...
you are watched over every moment of every day."*

Life is a Journey!

to live that adventure and ride that wild ride. You all reach your destinies in due time—all with a plan, all with a map, all with a compass. You simply have to use the tools that you have been given, watch the road, stay awake and hold on for dear life. Life IS dear and precious! It is a glorious journey that must be taken.

Why sit in your driveway?...It may feel safe, but what fun would that be? If a tree is going to fall, it is going to fall. You cannot escape it if it is meant to land on you...So why not see the world and live the adventure? Cherish every moment and make every moment count. Take control of the wheel and steer in the direction that you would like to go. Put your foot on the gas and let her rip. Let the breeze blow through your hair and fly like the wind. Do not be afraid to journey and discover. If you get lost simply take out your compass and find your direction again.

"Life is a journey and a mystery that is meant to be traveled and unraveled. Journey forth... seeking the truths of life and the purpose of your path."

There is no harm in discovery, only harm in not living or in not trying to find the right path. Life is a journey and a mystery that is meant to be traveled and unraveled. Journey forth on this road to joy and enlightenment, stretching far into the distance, seeking the truths of life and the purpose of your path. You are meant to travel this gifted road to awareness and self-discovery. Self-discovery is the journey of a lifetime—your lifetime! Treasure it! Enjoy it! Live it!

"Self-discovery is the journey of a lifetime—your lifetime!"

> *"Things must be revealed and unburied in order to discover their true meaning and purpose. Once discovered... the journey has begun and the path has been changed."*

July 3, 2009 (47 minutes)

Unearth Your Purpose & Your Path

I shall now speak to you of the wisdom that comes forth from the greater depths of the soul and not from the mind which is clouded by the fallen shadows of time. I feel the need to remind you of your purpose, that which has been long forgotten with your birth into this realm of time and space. This true reality is lost to your conscious mind and is buried beneath the recesses of thought and the wasteful ponderings of wonder. Keep your eyes focused on what you need to see, not what dwells beneath the weight of the world. There should be no doubt as to the glory that lies beyond this visible reality of Earth.

> *"Life is a gift and it is being given—but you must grasp it and unwrap it, experience it and cherish it."*

Life is a gift and it is being given—but you must grasp it and unwrap it, experience it and cherish it. Live in the moment, the moment that mixes time and space into a whirlwind of opportunity which exists like no other. There is not a single moment in life that has no purpose, for the purpose lies not only at the surface but digs its roots deep into the soil burying and burrowing like a mole digs its home. Think outside the

Unearth Your Purpose & Your Path

box. Pop off the lid and look inside, then remove its contents in order to fully examine and utilize the gift within. Things must be revealed and unburied in order to discover their true meaning and purpose. Once discovered, there is no going back as the journey has begun and the path has been changed.

"The answers will be clear when the time is right, but the work and toil come nevertheless."

 A mole has its path—one that may be underground, but it is still a path, no less or no more. You are all equal and all serve out your purposes. Just as the mole buries his head underground, you too must play out your part and follow your path digging deep when required to do so, or reaching up into the Light when you are called forth. The answers will be clear when the time is right, but the work and toil come nevertheless. Do not judge the task by the dirt that is dredged up or by the soil that is toiled. It is not for you to judge the mole or his dirty job—it is his job and his birthright. It is not for you to say that it is right or wrong, clean or dirty, desirable or undesirable. Let the mole dig his hole and you dig OUT of yours.

Watch where you walk, watch where you climb. Succumb to your every whim, for those whims will stretch you to new heights and launch you to new dreams—dreams of discovery and growth. Do not be afraid to push and unbury your head. Keep it out of the dirt and lift your face to the sky. Do not be like the mole whose eyes become accustomed to the dark; that may be his destiny but not yours. You are to shine in the Light and grow in the Sun, allowing the waters of the Earth to wash over you and cleanse your soul. Nourish your thoughts with those of sunlight and flowers, birds and honey. Peace will come out of the blue skies and fresh air, not from the darkness of the Earth's recesses or the recesses of your mind.

> *"Freedom is the key, the key to all. Freedom is found not in the mind-play but rather in the song of the heart."*

> *"Live to journey and journey to live..."*

Freedom is the key, the key to all. Freedom is found not in the mind-play but rather in the song of the heart. Sing sweetly, my child, for in the melody of Earth's music plays out the mystery of wonder and joy. Discover what is to be discovered. Live to journey and journey to live—that is all that is important, that is all that is necessary. Breathe in the night air and feel the glow of the moonlight, for nature stirs the imagination giving way to dreams and creating a new world of wonder and Light. Do not let the magic die in your mind, but let it launch within your heart.

> *"Expectation is what creates. If you expect it and feel it, it will become reality. Change the direction of your thoughts; turn onto a new path and the outcome will also change."*

Expectation is what creates. If you expect it and feel it, it will become reality. Change the direction of your thoughts; turn onto a new path and the outcome will also change. What you can conceive of will be. Expect the best and the best will be. Every moment creates anew—manifest what you desire. It is all within your hands, as it is within the hands of all. Simply imagine the power within as it is yours to utilize and create. The time is now and it is ALWAYS now—it is never too late, it is never lost. As long as you are alive, you have the power to direct your Earthly journey and discover your own wondrous abilities.

Once you realize your God-given gifts you can begin to reap the rewards. Struggle and strife bring you to this realization...How else would these

> *"Once you realize your God-given gifts you can begin to reap the rewards. Struggle and strife bring you to this realization."*

> *"It is a gift to have suffered, a great gift that brings a deep understanding that stamps into the soul and transcends beyond this lifetime alone—one that lasts an eternity and strengthens the soul of the world, the soul of the masses."*

gifts be discovered if you had not taken the time due to discontent and turmoil of the heart? Heartbreak is what brings the desire to mend and heal. To soothe the wound brings an understanding and a compassion for those that dwell outside—those that need the help of others to heal. It is a gift to have suffered, a great gift that brings a deep understanding that stamps into the soul and transcends beyond this lifetime alone—one that lasts an eternity and strengthens the soul of the world, the soul of the masses.

Do not suffer for the suffering of others as that suffering is necessary for the greater good of the Universe and the understanding of the godly ways of Earthbound plight. Once the suffering is done, things can transcend and transform the plight of mankind. To suffer is necessary for some, but does not have to be touched upon by others. Each of you has roles to play out and paths to choose. You do not have to choose a path of suffering—you have freewill.

Release your detrimental beliefs into the wind and let them fly away, never to land upon you again. Let your soul soar and lift you above all that has pulled and weighed you down. Release those mind-nagging beliefs that are simply an illusion that creates your reality. Create a new reality, one that appeals to your inner soul and blossoms from within. Be at peace with yourself and create your life as you would like to see it.

> *"...stay in the present on your current path...*
> *There are always other paths to distract and beckon,*
> *but those are NOT the paths that you are on*
> *so do not jump around in your mind."*

Time will tell you where to journey. For now, stay in the present on your current path. Be where you are and do not wander aimlessly in the dark, searching and feeling your way into chaos. The path may wind and narrow, but it always brings you to an adventure worth traveling—after all, life is a journey of discovery and growth with its challenges and beauty, its detours and streams. Ride the rivers and climb the mountains, slide down the hills and smell the roses, but be where you are and not looking for a new path. There are always other paths to distract and beckon, but those are NOT the paths that you are on so do not jump around in your mind.

Learn now so that you can be a tool for your children, a reference point to spring from. Help them launch their dreams and seek higher roads for them to travel so that they too can launch their own children and the world to come. You are all launching pads for each other and for the next generations. You are to help the journeys of each other but not to interfere with another's growth.

> *"You are all launching pads for each other and for the*
> *next generations. You are to help the journeys of each other*
> *but not to interfere with another's growth."*

September 5, 2009 (51 minutes)

Unravel Your Truth & Spin Your Dream

Feel the presence of God the Almighty and the Light that He projects forth, dispelling all that unrests the souls of mankind. Awaken to the peace and wisdom of His teachings, allowing that knowledge to seep through your being and into your soul. Watch and await the messages to unravel like mysteries of time-traveled wonders being read through the mind's eye—through the greater vision of your being.

Mankind has set forth to discover and learn and uncover the truths of the Universe. All shall be revealed as man opens up to these teachings and lessons. All is a mystery that awaits permission to be discovered and explored. You must allow the vision to unfold, setting forth a new path to be discovered and journeyed upon, but this path unwinds only when it is walked upon—leading forth into a forest thick with knowledge and truth, magic of discovery, and visions beyond man's wildest dreams. Let destiny set you upon this path by opening your mind's eye to this wonder and magical, mystical adventure, for in its discovery lie the answers and supreme power of God the Almighty. He is there to lead when you ask and when you seek to follow your dreams into the wonder and wisdom of learning—for the Light of God awaits you to beckon His presence, calling upon His greater knowledge and wisdom.

"You can only journey forth when you set your sights to do so. If you simply sit and await an adventure of discovery, it shall never appear."

> *"Laziness cannot set in, not here on Earth where the lessons are hard and the vision is hindered."*

You can only journey forth when you set your sights to do so. If you simply sit and await an adventure of discovery, it shall never appear. The work must be done and your hands must toil in order to bring about the journey that is meant to be. Laziness cannot set in, not here on Earth where the lessons are hard and the vision is hindered. Rise to the occasion, rise to the wonder. Lift your sights and lift your soul. Discover what you have come to this Earth to do. Discover it through discipline of the mind and vision of the soul. Discover in wonder as your life unfolds when you simply allow it to.

> *"Once you have found what you are seeking, you will realize that you had previously been lost only to your own hidden resources and the wisdom and wonder of God."*

Do not get trapped in despair or trickery of the mind which plays games of "Hide and Seek" and "Lost and Found". The mind is deceptive and has its own agenda, creating moments of loss and times of trouble. Set yourself free and allow the wisdom to flow through your heart—that is from where truth and vision emerge. You may feel lost at times, but you are never truly lost, only stuck in the muck of despair created by the ponderings of your mind. Cut those losses and find yourself by redirecting your purpose and seeking the path to discovery. Once you have found what you are seeking, you will realize that you had previously been lost only to your own hidden resources and the wisdom and wonder of God.

> *"Unravel your OWN truth to discover YOUR dream!"*

Unravel Your Truth & Spin Your Dream

You must seek to understand your own truth as there are many aspects and interpretations to life, just as a Bible is understood only when translated by man—yet it can be translated in so many different ways, interpreted until the "truth be told" for the bearer of the message or the reader of the dream. Unravel your OWN truth to discover YOUR dream! Journey forth into this discovery to unravel the mystery of your life and the puzzle of your path. Walk into this mystery and discover what your soul longs to pull forth out of this lifetime of hardship and pain—for in pain comes wisdom and through wisdom comes a life of servitude to mankind and a lifting of yourself and your brothers toward the Light of God and His wondrous vast teachings and healings, mysteries and magic.

"Dreams are meant to be discovered and launched, not meant to lie in sleep waiting to be awakened from within."

Walk forth and wait no more, for in waiting comes strife and incomplete dreams. Dreams are meant to be discovered and launched, not meant to lie in sleep waiting to be awakened from within. You must give rise to those dreams, weave them and spin them into a web of beauty and wonder that sparkles in the sunlight and dances in the wind.

> A spider spins her web of wonder with a thread of silk, suspended in the air of her dreams. She is strong and her web is mighty. It nourishes her need to create and feeds her soul, entrapping all that invade her precious territory. Her web is her castle, her dream, her home. It provides and protects, leaving her to peacefully create her life simply out of thin air and hope, knowingness and wonder. What magic she spins forth, weaving her web and living her purpose and her dream. Her life is simple and it is easy. It is carefree and requires little effort. Her web-spinning is God-given and what is created is a mystery of great beauty and miraculous strength. It provides all that is necessary to support her needs and sustain her life.

Spin your web, your web of wonder—one that suits your needs and glistens in the Light of God. Let the dew drops dance and play upon your heartstrings and threads of hope. Let the sunlight shine through and shine brightly upon the artistry that you weave.

> *"Create your life through the purpose that calls*
> *from within your heart, and trust*
> *that God has given you the resources to do so."*

> *"Listen to the inner whisperings of your heart*
> *and feel the tug of the strings that pull at your soul.*
> *They will nudge you in the direction of the path*
> *that you were set on Earth to take.*
> *Walk that fine line to discovery and weave the wonder*
> *and beauty that only you can create."*

Just as the spider dances along the path that it weaves, you too are meant to dance along your path—the path that you weave and set forth upon. Create your life through the purpose that calls from within your heart, and trust that God has given you the resources to do so. Just as the spider knows her purpose, you also do. Listen to the inner whisperings of your heart and feel the tug of the strings that pull at your soul. They will nudge you in the direction of the path that you were set on Earth to take.

Walk that fine line to discovery and weave the wonder and beauty that only you can create. Be that spider of supreme strength and agility. Walk high above the Earth building bridges that connect destinations which reach beyond and stretch forth into the distance. Trust, and you will be guided and you will be protected. God awaits your arrival and discovery of that purpose which beckons your approval to proceed. He is there to assist you and net your fall if need be.

Just as the spider can walk upon her own sticky creation without getting ensnared, you too will master your own mystery without getting stuck when you discover your true calling within. Let your life take shape when you weave your path to discover the beauty that you can create through unraveled mysteries that spring forth from your heart. You are an artist in your own right. Simply begin to spin your own web for all to revel in, and watch the magical transformation take place in your life.

"Just as the spider can walk upon her own sticky creation without getting ensnared, you too will master your own mystery without getting stuck when you discover your true calling within."

"You are all treasures—gifts from God & of God—& you are meant to live as God, bringing Light to this Earth & to each other. You are not to hinder each other's growth but to nourish each other's souls—transforming the Earth..."

July 25, 2009 (60 minutes)

Weave Your Life's Tapestry with Joy

The messages that I bring are for the good of mankind and are spoken through me to you from God the Almighty. Watch and listen to learn of the pattern that brings forth the coming change in the Earthly movement of life. Let go of the past and all of its holds that trap and twist at your soul. Come forth out of the darkness and into the Light and together we shall bring a new dawn of brightness. Lost are the souls that cannot see the Light; they will lie in darkness until they open their eyes and remove the filters that have trapped them in a time capsule of struggle and strife. The dawn of a new day shall arise, unearthing the souls that stretch toward the Light.

Listen to the whispers of the wind, the messages that ride upon the clouds of Heaven. Divinely sent are these messages, for they are directly from God. How quickly transformation can take place once you open your eyes and heart allowing the wisdom of God to flood your presence with Light and love. The Sun washes the Earth in Light. Lift your face to this shining glory and you will see what awaits your soul, for with the bright Light comes the messages and meaning of life and love—an awakening to the godly spirit that resides in all.

Weave Your Life's Tapestry with Joy

You are all treasures—gifts from God and of God—and you are meant to live as God, bringing Light to this Earth and to each other. You are not to hinder each other's growth but to nourish each other's souls—transforming the Earth, creating paths of lush growth and prosperity, abundance and joy. Do not walk a crooked and bent path that twists and turns into the darkness but rather a straight one that leads directly into the Light, lifting your soul to its limitless potential.

"You are not meant to suffer & toil, to strain & wallow over lost causes, but rather to fly free & soar to new heights."

You are not meant to suffer and toil, to strain and wallow over lost causes, but rather to fly free and soar to new heights. Let go of all that has trapped your soul in the past—all that has been lost and forgotten. Walk swiftly up the road and into a new beginning, a new day. Each moment creates a new opportunity for growth and ascent—a lifting of your soul to new heights, launching dreams of golden opportunity, for God is your keeper, and you shall walk hand-in-hand with Him along this golden road of Light.

Do not let the shadows fall upon you as the forest thickens into the dusk, for the shadows lock away the key to your growth and shut the doors of opportunity that shine in the glory ahead. Watch closely where you walk so as not to trip over branches that stem from the Earth. These gnarled and knotted roots can trip you up, creating stumbling blocks that hinder your progress and prolong your journey. The shadows from the past and the roots that bind, block the progress of your soul's ascent. When the

"The shadows from the past & the roots that bind, block the progress of your soul's ascent. When the darkness is shone with Light, these all but disappear clearing the way for quicker steps toward brighter days & new growth."

darkness is shone with Light, these all but disappear clearing the way for quicker steps toward brighter days and new growth. Launch your soul toward the brighter path, and with ease and swiftness your ascent will be—bringing you to days of glory and skies of sunshine.

In the hollows of your mind play the tricks that mankind has performed and separated into the whimsical "realities" of life. These mind-created realities are false fronts and hindrances to man's true potential—a potential which is a limitless reflection and refraction of God's image. Act as a prism, shining the Light of God's intent.

"Do not trap yourself by the limits and the history of man's thinking, but seek higher ground."

Do not trap yourself by the limits and the history of man's thinking, but seek higher ground. The earth you walk upon has no bearing upon the future of days to come. The actual future lies within your own hands and is placed therein by the vision within your mind's eye. Look forth to see what potential lies ahead. Look toward the Light, toward the messages of God, and into your mind's eye will spring a wealth of opportunity and a road filled with riches—riches of the heart and soul, riches of growth and joy and prosperity.

"...to hinder another's path is to hinder your own, stopping the progress dead in its tracks."

"Once the journey is filled with joy and release, the richness of the texture will take shape creating a tapestry of artistry and beauty—a life full of richness uniquely patterned to your individual soul's destiny."

Weave Your Life's Tapestry with Joy

Weave through life a tapestry, creating a path of rich color and texture—one that follows your soul's true vision and desire. Do not hinder the progress by getting caught and knotted by resentment and jealousy, for to hinder another's path is to hinder your own, stopping the progress dead in its tracks. Weave your own path and do not crisscross over another's, for this spoils the beauty of your own life—delaying and embarking upon a journey not meant to be. Let go of resentment, for that has no purpose but rather spoils the fun and joy that is meant to shine through. Joy is the goal. It is the purpose of the path, the purpose of the journey. Once the journey is filled with joy and release, the richness of the texture will take shape creating a tapestry of artistry and beauty—a life full of richness uniquely patterned to your individual soul's destiny.

Treasure your path and your tapestry of life, for it is unique to you, created by your journey and your soul's choosing. Do not doubt that this is all within your control. You choose what stitches to make, what colors to weave, what scene to portray and the speed at which your vision transforms. It is all at your fingertips awaiting your direction.

---

*"Treasure your path and your tapestry of life,
for it is unique to you, created by
your journey and your soul's choosing.
Do not doubt that this is all within your control."*

Your path is quickened or delayed by the progress in your mind's eye—the vision that stands out awaiting the Light from beyond. Do not cloud your judgment by not looking toward the Light but by glancing back at the shadows of time. This will only fog your path hindering the progress in reaching your soul's ultimate destiny and joy.

Focus on the task at hand and weave the life that is meant to be—an artistry of your lineage and your soul. Do not walk through the forest of shadows, for in this thicket lies only darkness and fear. There is no darkness and there is no fear when the Light is allowed to shine through your mind, reaching in to illuminate your soul's true purpose and glory, for within your reach is a wealth of abundance and joy.

"Focus on the task at hand and weave the life that is meant to be—an artistry of your lineage and your soul."

"You have come to the Earth for purposes that can only be revealed through struggle and strife. These purposes...are there to transform your soul into enlightenment...unfolding man as a whole into a supreme being of magnificent beauty and Light."

August 29, 2009 (60 minutes)

Piece Together the Greater Picture

Let go and release your troubles; let your soul fly free and discover the power that resides in all. Comfort awaits those that look to the heavens for answers and "Behold!", an answer will appear right before your very eyes—an answer filled with the wisdom of golden Light lifted upon wings of hope and prayer. I am here to deliver these messages to inform the world of this greater gift of truth.

"The minds of the world must be put at ease in order to open them up to the Light that shines forth into the dawning and unfolding of the Earth."

The minds of the world must be put at ease in order to open them up to the Light that shines forth into the dawning and unfolding of the Earth. Open upon a new time of growth and discovery, Light and love, and into the hearts and minds and souls of Earth's dwellers shall enter answers and enlightenment, wisdom and rebirth. Sorrow shall be dissolved and pain dispelled, strife shall be banished and burdens relinquished. Walk hand-in-hand with your brothers and watch the Sun rise to brighter days and glory.

> *"When man releases his limits and realizes his own power—that power that surfaces and springs forth through the callings and yearnings within—he will realize his true full-potential."*

You have come to the Earth for purposes that can only be revealed through struggle and strife. These purposes unfold without warning and are there to transform your soul into enlightenment. All souls are meant to be transformed and progressed—unfolding man as a whole into a supreme being of magnificent beauty and Light. Love abounds and has no bounds, but is an ever-expanding vision of God's purpose and prayer of hope. When man releases his limits and realizes his own power—that power that surfaces and springs forth through the callings and yearnings within—he will realize his true full-potential.

Supreme power is sparked and kindled through the flame of God's breath and the life force of love. Nurturing and cherishing sparks this in all. Just as the flower unfolds to the Light of the Sun, humanity unfolds to the Light and love of God and the cherishing and nurturing of all that is God and all that God created.

> *"Set forth upon a different path, one that nurtures and encourages growth within the self as well as in others… That is what sparks the being within and smolders out the discontent and worry…"*

When you set out to harm, you dim that Light within—pulling down your power and harming yourself as well as the one you set forth to hurt and drag down. There is no purpose in that and all that comes is destruction and angst. Set forth upon a different path, one that nurtures and encourages growth within the self as well as in others. That is what waters and feeds the soul. That is what sparks the being within and

"Weep not and fear not, for there is ALWAYS hope. There are always answers and complete and continuous healing offered through the Universe."

smolders out the discontent and worry that distracts and beckons you to follow and stumble upon the wrong, dark and fearful path—a journey that is not meant to be taken.

Brighten your life and the world around you by calling upon the gifts granted by God, for to open up to these gifts is to open up to a magnificent world showered with hope and wonder which springs forth with abundance and joy. Weep not and fear not, for there is ALWAYS hope. There are always answers and complete and continuous healing offered through the Universe. Ask and open up to the gifts that fill the atmosphere with cherished, all-knowing truth and power.

Prepare for a life of luxury and health, wealth, love and abundance. That is your right and it is the right of all. You simply must allow it to be and allow it to shine forth unconditionally upon all the souls of mankind. Do not dim this gifted Light of God—the gift which is meant to shine upon all—that Light which is pure and clear of fear and jealousy, revenge and angst.

"You are meant to create and grow, not stifle and struggle. Do not hold others back, dragging yourself behind, leaving yourself covered in dust with unclean hands."

Power is lost when it is used to conquer and control, hoard and scavenge. Power blossoms when the breath of love and Light are exhaled and spread outward to the Universe, giving birth to new ideas and creation. You are meant to create and grow, not stifle and struggle. Do not hold others back, dragging yourself behind, leaving yourself covered in dust with unclean hands. Wash your soul with the Light of God, filling the void within yourself and showering the Earth with love. You will benefit from the growth that springs forth from your own creation of spirit, and the Earth will blossom in delight. A transformation will take place within your own life as well as those around you. All will be good, all will be grand, all will dwell in glory within the Kingdom of God.

You are all meant to stand tall and shine forth, reflecting and basking in the glow of God and each other. You are not meant to dwell in darkness smothering each other's flames of truth and justice. Behold and shine. Love and live. Let go and let God through your all-knowing, all-powerful Light of being. Shine that Light and shine brightly, glowing with love for all and glory for God. Filter your thoughts and relinquish your pain, allowing life to unfold with the godly expanse of the heavens. Beacon to all your purpose for living—that which is granted through God and that which is given unto you for the purpose of shining forth, encompassing all in love and allowance for being.

"Free yourself from the burdens of your mind and the pains of the past, for those pains block your soul and give rise to fear. That fear twists and turns your spirit with anger that gets directed toward yourself and others..."

Free yourself from the burdens of your mind and the pains of the past, for those pains block your soul and give rise to fear. That fear twists and turns your spirit with anger that gets directed toward yourself and others—anger that is rooted deeply. But those roots can be cut, severing the hold that binds you to your pain. Call forth upon God and your inner strength to break those bonds and free you—free you and set you onto the path which you are meant to travel, for the travel is slow if you are dragged down and bound strongly to your inner thoughts and the demons of your mind.

Piece Together the Greater Picture

*"Through prayer and meditation the healing can begin,
breaking the bonds and tearing down the walls
that block your progress and
keep you from traveling forth upon your destined road."*

Through prayer and meditation the healing can begin, breaking the bonds and tearing down the walls that block your progress and keep you from traveling forth upon your destined road. Be a beacon for yourself, Lighting the way and shining forth for others to follow. Lead yourself out of the darkness and brighten the path of tomorrow.

*"Lessons are learned through trial and error. As long as
the lesson is learned, that path or journey was not in error."*

Do not be haunted by your past or the mistakes and pains of your human life. Life is a difficult journey and is a path meant to be traveled with discovery and growth. Lessons are learned through trial and error. As long as the lesson is learned, that path or journey was not in error.

Do not berate yourself for those past "mistakes" of the path—for there are no mistakes, simply bits and pieces of a puzzle, a greater picture that is revealed one piece at a time. Sometimes one must try to fit various pieces into the puzzle until it is discovered which piece is correct. There is no error in "trial and error" if the truth is discovered and the lesson is learned.

The puzzle pieces all begin to take shape and form a more complete picture as your life's journey is played out—but you must play the game. Fit in the pieces—take a chance—or your life will not take shape. The puzzle will not put ITSELF together, and there is nothing wrong or incorrect about piecing your life together one piece, or lesson, at a time. But do avoid trying to shove the same piece in over and over again. Do not dwell or rehash something about your life that just does not, or did not fit into place. Simply move on and try a different piece. Discover what the bigger picture will reveal as you journey to discover yourself and the mystery of life, one piece at a time—one tiny bit of your magnificent being—one puzzle piece at a time.

"Discover what the bigger picture will reveal as you journey to discover yourself and the mystery of life, one piece at a time—one tiny bit of your magnificent being—one puzzle piece at a time."

November 9, 2009 (37 minutes)

Cherish Yourself

At those times when you feel lost inside yourself and kicked to the wayside by others, you are trapped within the recesses of your mind in a state of self-doubt and self-denial. Your heart has been vandalized with graffiti written all over it. You must wash it clean and let the damage run down the drain—where it belongs. Free yourself from the limited thinking of others, as their opinions do not matter. They are not the final judge or ruler of you or your fate—you are and God is. God is your witness and you must please only yourself and Him. He has a plan envisioned and honors your highest-good and higher-purpose.

"Mind only your good opinion of yourself and remain focused upon that—not upon the self-incriminating chatterings of your mind or upon the expectations or criticisms of others."

Mind only your good opinion of yourself and remain focused upon that—not upon the self-incriminating chatterings of your mind or upon the expectations or criticisms of others. Wash yourself clean of these influences and let them slide away in a swirling drain of waste, for that is all that is accomplished with such negative thoughts and self-accusations—waste to your self, waste to your time, and waste to your soul and self-esteem.

It is time to take control and take action to get yourself on course. Pull yourself up by the bootstraps and let the waste and drainage be gone.

"...you are a child of God and you are meant to shine..."

Rise up from the dust of your mind and feel the self-love in your heart. Focus on the positive aspects of you—those that you treasure and those that shine brightly. As you see those, you will begin to see other aspects which will help lift you into the Light—the Light of God. Let yourself shine in this Light for all to see, without a care of judgment or recrimination, for you are a child of God and you are meant to shine—whether you have the belief and confidence in yourself, or not. With God at your side, together you will lift your spirits, enabling your Light to shine forth.

"Without heartfelt communication, another's circumstances are often misinterpreted or go unnoticed— getting buried beneath the observer's own burdens."

It need not matter if others understand you—only that you understand yourself. Others have a hard enough time examining and focusing upon their own lives, that they get lost in the chaos of that. Humans often lack insight and sensitivity, understanding and compassion, and do not communicate with the heart. Without heartfelt communication, another's circumstances are often misinterpreted or go unnoticed—getting buried beneath the observer's own burdens. Their eyes do not see past their own noses and into the eyes and souls of others. They have closed the doors and blinds, shutting themselves off, in order to hide their own hurts and protect themselves from being forced into change and potentially painful growth. Be your own nurturer and your own provider, relishing and cherishing the beautiful soul that your are.

"Do not allow the blind eyes of others to define who you are. Do not allow the hardened or closed hearts of others to damage and vandalize your own heart with their warped paintings of you."

Cherish Yourself

Do not block your own Light and ability to grow and shine forth, by placing your worth in the hands of others. Do not allow the blind eyes of others to define who you are. Do not allow the hardened or closed hearts of others to damage and vandalize your own heart with their warped paintings of you.

"You are the only one that defines who you are—you hold the brush and the control is in your hands. Paint a glorious picture of your own creation, and create your own worth."

 Define yourself, and believe in that definition. Paint your own picture and your own life with the beautiful gifts and Light that God has bestowed upon you. You are the only one that defines who you are—you hold the brush and the control is in your hands. Paint a glorious picture of your own creation, and create your own worth. It does not matter if anyone interprets you inaccurately. All that matters is that you paint your own glory to radiate forth into the world.

Do not hide your portrait in the attic or in the dark recesses of your mind, afraid for others to see. What good does it do hiding away in the dark? How then can it come to be and affect the world as intended? How can you do your part and shine your glory if you remain in hiding, afraid to show your true colors? Let your colors shine, and do so proudly. There is no other you—and there is not supposed to be. You have your Light and beauty and have your place in the world—as have all other inhabitants of the Earth. Do not block your own Light and do not block the Light of others by lying in judgment of your own, or another's, painted glory. You are all meant to shine your own Light and reflect the Light of God—creating a glorious world of combined Light and artistry.

"Everyone shines forth in different ways, but no one is any more important or any more valid than anyone else. Everyone simply has different strengths and different weaknesses, different gifts and different lessons."

Let yourself shine forth and realize that others also struggle and hide who they really are—afraid to reveal their true selves. Some of you are bolder than others, some shine more gently, some are more rigid, some more flexible. Everyone shines forth in different ways, but no one is any more important or any more valid than anyone else. Everyone simply has different strengths and different weaknesses, different gifts and different lessons. You must all shine forth in order to teach each other and in order to serve as an example—allowing and enabling others to also shine with confidence, knowing that it is everyone's right and purpose to do so.

"God knows of your purpose, your flight and journey— believe in yourself as God does and release your spirit so that it can soar to new heights."

Nurture your own beautiful heart and cherish it dearly, cradling it within your being as if it were a tiny bird. Your spirit resides within and is delicate—easily damaged and gentle in nature. Release that gentle spirit from the burdens of your mind and the insensitivity of others. Release it from the pressures of Earth and let it fly free, knowing that God is the wind beneath its wings. God knows of your purpose, your flight and journey—believe in yourself as God does and release your spirit so that it can soar to new heights.

"Do not be afraid to shine differently, for that is the most magnificent of all artwork—that which shines in its own uniqueness and is not simply a replication of the masses."

When you feel trapped by burdened thoughts or the opinions of others, when you feel as if you do not fit in, or when you feel as though something is missing from your life, listen to your heart and not your head. Tune in to the center of your being—the place where God sits gently with your spirit—and know that you are not alone and that your soul-purpose is to shine forth with who you are. You are to shine forth with your Light and the Light of God in a brilliant combination that shines like no other, with its own unique colors and own unique artistry. Do not be afraid to shine differently, for that is the most magnificent of all artwork—that which shines in its own uniqueness and is not simply a replication of the masses. How would change and growth occur if everyone simply conformed to the thoughts and opinions of others?

Believe in yourself and the beauty that you are. You are a gift to the world, but you need to shine forth in order to make the difference that you are meant to make.

"You are a gift to the world, but you need to shine forth in order to make the difference that you are meant to make."

Section IV
God's Greater Wisdom & Ever-Presence

It is not about 'being right'. It is about 'getting it right'—stretching and growing toward your highest potential and blossoming into who you are meant to become. The Earth is a training ground and you are God's seeds. Water and feed your souls with God's Light and wisdom, spreading your own love and Light in order to bring paradise—a heaven on Earth. You are all meant to nurture and aid each other, growing toward your true potential as a species and not to cast shadows, blocking out the truth and Light of God, for you are His creation and His children and are meant to live as He intends with the gifts that He bestows upon you.

Rise and shine in His Light and walk the path to enlightenment, for nothing else matters. All is simply an illusion to nudge you forth onto the right path—into the journey of soul searching and the discovery of God and His wisdom, wonders and worldly creations. Rest assured that He will not fail and peace and love will prevail.

> "...use the heart and soul. That is the greatest gift that can be learned, the gift of insight and intuition—to know where to go and how to get there through the guidance of God."

April 2, 2009 (62 minutes)

God's Unfolding Truths

The answers to the mysteries of life will come to you from within—through God's wisdom as felt through your heart and as seen through your mind's eye. You have the power to see all that is, just as the world is capable of this greater vision—it simply has to be allowed to enter through the soul. Be at peace with the Earth's dawning and discovery, and the changes that are coming about. All is well when it is allowed to come into being.

> *"You, and all life, are connected to God—to this essence of creation. Once you settle within this peace and vibration, your life will flow with ease and unrestraint."*

The wisdom and presence of God is like a song sung through the heart, vibrating with the magic of the ocean and the pull of the moon. It fills the void where nothing else can. Resonate with this joyous music and feel the pull of the sea—the essence of God and His glory as experienced through nature and the rhythm of the Universe. You, and all life, are connected to God—to this essence of creation. Once you settle within this peace and vibration, your life will flow with ease and unrestraint.

Feel with your heart and turn off your mind. The heart is from where true inspiration and guidance come. This wisdom of the All-Knowing unlocks

> *"The heart is from where true inspiration and guidance come. This wisdom of the All-Knowing unlocks and reveals the truths and justices that serve mankind and all of life."*

and reveals the truths and justices that serve mankind and all of life. Within this realm of opportunity and enlightenment is a force and power greater than any other. It is all-encompassing and expansive and lifts the worries of the mind and unburdens and untraps the soul that is locked within, awaiting to discover and fulfill its greater glory and purpose in life.

This magical, mystical ever-powerful presence is limitless and ageless. It is ever clear in its knowing and Light and is boundless in its expanse and potential for creation. Through tapping into this magnificent resource of truth and discovery, abundance and love, all pain shall be dissolved—all hardship, all burden and all worry. Your life will unfold to the beauty of the Universe and its vast resources of growth and opportunity, wealth and power-of-being. Lift yourself up to this level of awareness—the level of God's truths—and your life will soar to new heights.

> *"There shall be no lack where there is true wisdom… where the mind is open and the soul is free…"*

Your ancestors set forth to create a boundless abundance of prosperity that is now coming to Light. Its potential is limitless. There shall be no lack where there is true wisdom—not wisdom of the mind but wisdom of the heart. There is a difference, one that is visibly clear, where the mind is open and the soul is free—free to journey through growth and compassion, love and truth. It is not bound by limits or lack, hate or fear. It is a paradise lost, but will soon be found.

Let love prosper within you, within your heart. Love yourself. See your beauty. See your strength. See your Light and believe in the magic of the

Universe—the magic of the moon, the mystery, and the joy of that mystery. You do not need to solve the riddles of the mind or the Universe. You simply need to open up to them. Open up to this mystery and allow it to be, allow it to happen. It is more fun that way and fun is what it is all about.

This greatness—this powerful presence—does not have to be analyzed, identified or figured out. It never will be! It is too vast, too expansive, too godly, too miraculous. Why bother? Then you are wasting that time which has been granted to experience, to live. Let life flow, let the wonder of it all be. Wonder not, worry not, live it up, lap it up, laugh it up—take it all in. That is what life is for. Simply experience it and expect it, then it will be. No worries, no stress, no pain, no lack. You need not know how, where or why. Just spread your wings and fly!

---

*"You need not know how, where or why.
Just spread your wings and fly!"*

---

*"Life unfolds like a butterfly...but there is a delicate balance
that can be destroyed by a powerful wind
that spins out of control, caused by distress of the soul."*

Life unfolds like a butterfly spreads its gossamer wings, catching the sunlight and floating on the breeze—but there is a delicate balance that can be destroyed by a powerful wind that spins out of control, caused by distress of the soul. It will beat down the beauty like a storm tearing at the delicate balance of life. Keep the winds calm and the sunlight sparkling through heartfelt wisdom and peace—then all is well. The butterfly will lift its head and soar to unbound heights, spreading its beauty in its flight. It will flit and float through life, sharing its gentle presence and awe with the Earth and its inhabitants. Life's journey is its purpose, seeing the world and experiencing its glory.

> *"...you are meant to allow your soul to fly free
> in a joyful flight of life—radiating and spreading
> your beauty throughout the world."*

Just as does the butterfly, you are meant to allow your soul to fly free in a joyful flight of life—radiating and spreading your beauty throughout the world. Stop and see the wonder. Smell the flowers. Bask in the Sun. For what else is there?....Only glory, only God, only love and Light, and its joy to behold. Love has no bounds or fears. And that is God—all that is good, all that is found. Not lost...Oh no, just the opposite. There is no loss when there is love to behold and feel. There is only Light, and its gifts that shine through to each individual that experiences it.

> *"...your heart speaks the truth as nothing else does.
> That is the center for all communication. That is the receiver
> of the unearthly voice that lives deep within your soul..."*

> *"Love is all there is. Anything else is an illusion
> that keeps you from centering and finding your true purpose.
> It is the time-waster, the destroyer,
> the culprit for unhealth and mismanagement of the mind."*

Feel from the heart—your heart speaks the truth as nothing else does. That is the center for all communication. That is the receiver of the unearthly voice that lives deep within your soul and the souls of all mankind. That is the voice of the Almighty, the Creator of the Universe, the Master of the Heavens. That is love. Love is all there is. Anything else is an illusion that keeps you from centering and finding your true purpose. It is the time-

> *"Earth sets limits that conform to the human mind. These limits alter man's perception of reality."*

waster, the destroyer, the culprit for unhealth and mismanagement of the mind. It is a detriment—a loss of self, and the higher-self and its ultimate purpose that strives to speak within your very being.

Earth sets limits that conform to the human mind. These limits alter man's perception of reality. Free yourself from these limitations and do not use the mind—use the heart and soul. That is the greatest gift that can be learned, the gift of insight and intuition—to know where to go and how to get there through the guidance of God. He knows all that is, and is wiser than any human, but you can be a tuning fork channeling this greater gift of awareness—this song of creation. You simply need to open up and be receptive to its vibrational path and attunement. Be that tuning fork, bringing in the Light of the Universe through God's gift of direction and meaning. Know no bounds. Live like you have never lived before and sing to the music of life. Prosper with the knowingness that you are of God—part of the infinite wisdom sent down through the ages, but with new purpose and vigor that is upon the dawning of enlightenment. It is a new age of wonder and wealth that is becoming the gift of life. All is now broken down so that it can build with new structure and purpose.

> *"Trust is key—no worry or concern, or having to know how."*

Simply open up your eyes—your mind's eye, the center of your vision—so that you can clear the way for life and joy. It takes discipline and work, but not much, just awareness and focus to bring clarity. Simply change your thought patterns and trust. Trust is key—no worry or concern, or having to know how. That is not necessary, but is detrimental to your opening to the vast expanse of Universal energy that must be allowed to flow through life's stream.

Jump into the flow, and venture forth to discover what you will pull forth from the vast wisdom of the Universe and the gifts of life. Fish away. Bait your line and toss it into the sea to see what you will catch. Cast far and deep into the recesses of your mind's eye in order to experience the mystery of what is limitless. Discover who you are through "true" life and joy in life. Do not hold back, as that will choke the line, and you will come up empty-handed with no fish to fry. Bask in the Sun. Feel the splash of the salt spray. Lap it up and live in the peaceful flow of life. Life is a joy—a gift that is meant to be utilized and cherished by you, God's child.

Walk on water and swim with the fish. Take glory in the rise of your spirit and the flight of your soul. Just as the seagull dips and dives and floats on the breeze, your spirit will also soar with the ebb and flow of the tide that whispers to the moon's shining glory. Life is an ever-unfolding mystery that changes through a timeless abundance of wealth and joy. It is not meant to drown the souls of the unfortunate that dwell in their own minds, but to bring forth enlightenment and peace.

Only through growth and learning does change occur. Peace is the goal, and peace shall come simply by opening to the opportunity to be guided by the Light of love and joy.

"Life is an ever-unfolding mystery that changes through a timeless abundance of wealth and joy. It is not meant to drown the souls of the unfortunate that dwell in their own minds, but to bring forth enlightenment and peace."

> *"God is the all-powerful, all-knowing source of all creation.
> ...Through prayer and focus,
> God's energy can be encompassed and heightened
> at any given time within any individual."*

November 1, 2010 (39 minutes)

God the Almighty

God is the all-powerful, all-knowing source of all creation. God lives and breathes out of love and Light and blows the breath of love and Light into every living soul. God encompasses all in an ever-expansion of creation, wisdom and Light—lifting all in a glory of manifestation. God is the seer of all, the creator of all, the orchestrator of all and the power of all.

Through prayer and focus, God's energy can be encompassed and heightened at any given time within any individual. God is always available offering assistance and guidance to all of His children...although free will reigns, and each child of God can choose to either harness this gifty energy of love and Light or turn his back and walk away toward darkness and negativity. Each individual has a choice, but it is God's desire and, therefore, the destined outcome to have all encompass love

> *"Each individual has a choice, but it is...the destined outcome to have all encompass love and Light. Those that turn away shall struggle with indecision and hardship, being drawn toward the energy that they are destined to encompass."*

and Light. Those that turn away shall struggle with indecision and hardship, being drawn toward the energy that they are destined to encompass.

There is choice for each individual within every moment of time, all of which lead him down his own path of discovery in order to arrive at his destined place in society—which is ultimately to harness God's energy and grace. God has the upper hand, one of powerful strength and control that wields its force, protecting those that strive toward good and grandness. He knocks the breath and life out of those that rise up against His energy, but not in a forceful, vengeful manner. Rather it is through lesson-teaching and nudging forth, striving to bring about results that shape and mold the individual into a loving, joyful, compassionate soul.

"...society is shaped and molded in a gradual process that lifts all toward the heightened awareness of mankind's heritage which is to inherit the Earth in a loving, giftful exchange of godly creation and manifestation."

If lessons ensue and learning fails, the lessons become heightened until the message is received and ingrained into the being of that soul. Upon that learning, society is shaped and molded in a gradual process that lifts all toward the heightened awareness of mankind's heritage which is to inherit the Earth in a loving, giftful exchange of godly creation and manifestation. The meek shall rise and the unwieldy shall fall. It is God's desire that this be expedited through the encompassment of God's wisdom and grace and into the knowing of every human being on Earth. That is why these writings and other messages are coming through for the betterment of mankind.

"Evil will not prosper, as that is not God's will, and God is the ruler of all and the creator of the Universe."

> *"When one's ego gets too large and the welfare of others is not taken into consideration, the more powerful lessons ensue, bringing man down to his knees in a prayer of surrender to God the Almighty."*

Evil will not prosper, as that is not God's will, and God is the ruler of all and the creator of the Universe. This all-powerful energy has laid down the laws that set the Universe into action, spinning the course for all to follow, pulling everything into alignment and launching dreams into reality. Doubt has been raised within the consciousness of mankind regarding the false conclusion that he himself is in control. When one's ego gets too large and the welfare of others is not taken into consideration, the more powerful lessons ensue, bringing man down to his knees in a prayer of surrender to God the Almighty. That is when the awareness of one's Creator takes place. This knowledge is revealed in bits and pieces until that individual becomes fully aware of his helplessness unless he encompasses the energy, wisdom and Light of God. That is when God's mighty strength and power is revealed, enabling that individual to truly live and breathe out of godly creation and manifestation.

If this great lesson of magnitude is not learned by that individual, he will continue to suffer hardship and pain in his current lifetime as well as in lifetimes to come, until the lesson is finally learned and he develops his soul into one that encompasses God's love and Light—cherishing all of creation.

> *"You are all One and are to live as One, encompassing God's energy and recognizing that which is of God's essence. Any opposing energy is to be rejected, dispelling its power and enabling its negativity to be replaced with God's rays of positivity and Light—locking out the darkness."*

> *"It is the choice of every individual to accept God's plan or to fight against it, but there is no sense fighting the All-Powerful when you...cannot possibly supersede His knowledge or power...It is against the laws of nature, and no human or human law can surpass or out rule that."*

You are all One and are to live as One, encompassing God's energy and recognizing that which is of God's essence. Any opposing energy is to be rejected, dispelling its power and enabling its negativity to be replaced with God's rays of positivity and Light—locking out the darkness. Man must rise together, first as individuals then in a banding of society in order to replace all of the negativity that resides upon the Earth. That is God's will, and that will be done. It is the choice of every individual to accept God's plan or to fight against it, but there is no sense fighting the All-Powerful when you are, in actuality, simply a small piece of God's Almighty wonder and cannot possibly supersede His knowledge or power no matter how large a force you muster up. It is against the laws of nature, and no human or human law can surpass or out rule that.

> *"You must let go and let God. Accept the wisdom and grace of the Almighty and allow your life to flow, seeing beyond the visible and thinking beyond the limited constraints that human society has taught you."*

You must let go and let God. Accept the wisdom and grace of the Almighty and allow your life to flow, seeing beyond the visible and thinking beyond the limited constraints that human society has taught you. All of the answers will appear if you will only ask and accept that which is revealed by God Himself and His angelic force of angels and enlightened

> *"With an individual's sincere desire to live through God and of-God, the guidance will appear and the help will ensue, lifting that individual toward the life that he is meant to live—one of joy and prosperity, peace and love."*

individuals. The vehicle for this is prayer—a prayer that speaks to God out of sincerity and motivation toward love and truth. With an individual's sincere desire to live through God and of-God, the guidance will appear and the help will ensue, lifting that individual toward the life that he is meant to live—one of joy and prosperity, peace and love.

> *"God is an ever-expansive energy that will not fail, that is all-knowing, and has every individual's highest good in mind. This seer-of-all orchestrates into reality the nudging forth of each individual toward his optimal growth into becoming who he is meant to be."*

God is an ever-expansive energy that will not fail, that is all-knowing, and has every individual's highest good in mind. This seer-of-all orchestrates into reality the nudging forth of each individual toward his optimal growth into becoming who he is meant to be. God's motivations are not to be questioned, but are to be understood. A mere mortal cannot see all that there is to see and must simply trust that he is on the path that he is meant to travel.

The key to success and development is striving to live a life out of love and goodness, fairness and truth—seeking the attainment of your best self. Keeping this in mind, you will reach your destined self at a much quicker pace and will be launched into your flight to freedom, able to shine your true self without fear or reserve. With the shining of each individual soul, God will radiate in all His glory, encompassing the Earth in a rainbow of Light that dances upon the waters of time. If a soul chooses to dim his Light and walk toward the darkness, he will not play a part in the magnificence that is to come. He will not shine in the kingdom of God's heavenly glory.

God is an energy of pure love, Light, power and strength and is neither male nor female. This energy has in the traditional sense been referred to as "Father" or "He" due to its powerful strength and might. The terminology in this book is simply that which flows through the receiver of these messages and speaks more clearly to a mass audience.

"The key to success and development is striving to live a life out of love and goodness, fairness and truth— seeking the attainment of your best self."

"Those that do not encompass this giftly Light will wilt and wither...Those of the Light shall blossom and bloom, creating rainbow-beauty throughout the Earth, living in harmony and dancing upon the waters of time."

September 18, 2009 (55 minutes)

The Light of God

I shall now speak of the all-encompassing Light of God. Feel within your soul the beginnings that take root, spreading and reaching out toward the Light of day. Watch in wonder and in glory as the rays of the Sun brighten each dawning day, stretching forth the existence of mankind and all earthly inhabitants. The Sun rises and it sets in perfect sequence and harmony, creating a picture-perfect portrait of colorful hues that warm the heart, body and soul. It shines forth, emitting rays of warmth and beams of Light that spark the growth and development of all.

Without the Sun there would be nothing. Just as without God, there would be no Sun. For the continuing survival of all, there must a Sun continue to rise. If the Sun continues to shine forth, then there must be a God orchestrating that miracle of Light and natural wonder—for in Light is God and in God is all of creation resting in beauty and rising in harmony, fortifying the growth and survival of those inhabitants of Earth.

"...in Light is God and in God is all of creation resting in beauty and rising in harmony, fortifying the growth and survival of those inhabitants of Earth."

Just as the Sun shall rise, so too shall the dawning of mankind. He will rise and shine forth in God's image and Light, gifting the Earth with the riches of his own reflective energy of God. Those that do not encompass this giftly Light will wilt and wither, just as a dying flower returns to the Earth and lies in peace in her dusty grave. Those of the Light shall blossom and bloom, creating rainbow-beauty throughout the Earth, living in harmony and dancing upon the waters of time. Peace will come throughout the Kingdom, reflecting and nurturing the Light of God, giving and receiving in harmony of this all-encompassing richness of the world.

"...a new day...lies in wait for the awakening of the souls of mankind. For once awakened, sleep shall no longer prevail and there will no longer be a lack of love and beauty, abundance and joy."

"Unravel the mysteries of the Universe through the realization of what you are—a true reflection of God's painted glory...meant to shine forth in love and creation in a giving exchange that abounds out of selfless sharing and nurturing hearts."

Float forth into the night and awaken with the dawning of the day—a new day that lies in wait for the awakening of the souls of mankind. For once awakened, sleep shall no longer prevail and there will no longer be a lack of love and beauty, abundance and joy. Unravel the mysteries of the Universe through the realization of what you are—a true reflection of God's painted glory in all the Light and brightness that He intends, meant to shine forth in love and creation in a giving exchange that abounds out of selfless sharing and nurturing hearts.

> *"When the heart is lit with love, it shines brightly forth, breaking through the dark barriers and blockades of past pain and future strife."*

Behold and shine forth, creating the perfect balance of peace and tranquility, love and Light. Shine forth for all to see, reflecting the rays of the Sun and its Creator, for in God rises the Sun. Look ahead to bright skies and peaceful nights that live within the hearts of mankind. When the heart is lit with love, it shines brightly forth, breaking through the dark barriers and blockades of past pain and future strife. Take in the Light of the Sun—the Light of God—and hold it within your heart, releasing it forth to shine through your soul and dance upon the brotherhood of mankind and the waters of the Earth. Reflect that love, that love of God, and spread it throughout the land, for nothing lives without love and nurturing. It withers away and dies.

Find peace within through the Light of God—through the Sun and the Moon, the earth and the rain. Nurture this peace through the tranquility and awe in nature. All is visible in the natural wonders of the Universe, those natural wonders that give evidence of God's very existence. Learn from nature. Learn from the peaceful rhythm that reflects God's glory, radiating Light in all the rich hues of the Universe—painting with a palette of love and beauty. See yourself in this reflective Light. See yourself through God's eyes, as you are His creation. You are His painted glory.

You are a living legacy to God's creative and imaginative being, created in wonder and in awe. But you are much more than a simple picture

> *"You are a living legend creating and developing your own history and shaping the outcome of human development. Play your part and play it well."*

> *"All is made possible through the resources of God's Light, and all is made to live in perfect harmony—giving and receiving, replenishing and providing."*

of perfection. You are a living legend creating and developing your own history and shaping the outcome of human development. Play your part and play it well. Carve your stone and whittle your wood. Craft your picture and paint your dream. This is your life and it is there for the making. Treasure it and shine forth utilizing God's Light to manifest your greatest destiny. All is possible. All is made possible through the resources of God's Light, and all is made to live in perfect harmony—giving and receiving, replenishing and providing.

There shall be no lack when the love and Light of God are free to shine forth. Allow that to shine forth through you—it is crucial to the survival of yourself and mankind as a whole. You have a choice. Be careful what you choose, as the present way of life cannot continue for much longer. Mankind is creating his own lack and strangling out the abundance that is meant to live and breathe freely. Let go of the anger toward your brothers and allow the Light of God to heal all wounds, for in anger comes disease and disaster, loss and lack. Take back your Light and love of all, through the opening of your heart toward this greater goodness of all. Trust in the Universe and the almighty power of God, and allow yourself to heal and develop into a higher level of being—one that shines forth in knowing beauty, trust and love, allowing others to shine as freely, releasing and dissolving the pains of this earthly world.

> *"The Light of God is crucial to the enlightenment of humanity. It is necessary in order to lift mankind from its current place of burden, pain and complacency."*

The Light of God

> *"There is no darkness where Light is allowed to shine forth."*

There is no darkness where Light is allowed to shine forth. The Light washes away the pain, bathing it in an all-encompassing healing energy of God. It washes and it soothes and it reflects away the deeply-rooted ghosts of the past, dissolving fear and lack, pain and worry. Once you are clear of the negative, painful energy of the past, you can shine forth in perfect harmony with God's Light—expanding and combining your own Light to create an even-brighter energy that nurtures both humankind and the Earth. Reflect this brightly through living with love, dissolving all judgment and mistreatment of your brothers. The Light of God is crucial to the enlightenment of humanity. It is necessary in order to lift mankind from its current place of burden, pain and complacency.

Focus on and draw from this magnificence in order to heal and move forth into a greater, more peaceful existence. Time must be taken and effort must be made in order to develop the heart and quiet the mind. The heart is where the center of the Universe lives and where the Light of God remains. Shine brightly by bringing forth God's loving power and spreading it joyfully throughout the Earth. You must not dim your own Light through setting forth to harm another or through neglect of the Earth—the very place which sustains your life. Nurture yourself, nurture each other and nurture the Earth through the loving peaceful Light and energy of God. Be a catalyst for change—a catalyst that will help move mankind toward a brighter more peaceful level of loving existence.

> *"...effort must be made in order to develop the heart and quiet the mind. The heart is where the center of the Universe lives and where the Light of God remains."*

♡

> *"The Universe offers All That Is to mankind and*
> *every living, breathing wake of life—*
> *allowing for the development and enrichment of that life itself.*
> *Without Universal energy nothing would exist."*

September 30, 2009 (54 minutes)

Universal Energy

Let us delve into the mystery of the Universe and its ever-changing growth. Let yourself go and align your breath and the beat of your heart to the rhythm of the Universe. It expands and contracts with a vast depth that encompasses all of humanity and all of life itself. It includes the pull of gravity and the rotation of the planets, the breadth of life and the vastness of the atmosphere. It is ever-changing and ever-clear in its frequency and Light as it tunes the soul and lifts the mind.

The Universe encompasses all, as a whole, through God's direction. It creates and it destroys in a burst of Light and energy, transcending the waves of time and space. The Universe offers All That Is to mankind and every living, breathing wake of life—allowing for the development and enrichment of that life itself. Without Universal energy nothing would exist. All is anchored within it, revolving in rotation that keeps itself and its elemental parts in perfect balance. The gravitational force pulls all into alignment keeping pace with the clock of time. The stars and planets rotate and feed off the energy of each other and the Universal suns.

Keep time with the Universe and you keep time with your self, for the energy within the Universe resides within you. You are One—and All That Is is encompassed within you. See this in your mind's eye and feel

Universal Energy

> *"Focus is key in order to lift from the burdens of your mind and the force of gravity that pulls at your soul-trapped conscious self."*

the power of that Universal energy. With conscious choice, all can be dispersed or all can be gathered when you focus through your mind's eye and anchor through your soul.

Lift your being to a higher vibration through conscious effort, pulling forth from the energy of the heavens above. Lift yourself above the pull of the Earth's gravity and into a higher plane that offers freedom from the pressures and pulls that weigh your human experience down. This comes through the alignment of your self with the Universe through meditation and conscious effort. Focus is key in order to lift from the burdens of your mind and the force of gravity that pulls at your soul-trapped conscious self.

> *"When you are unconscious through sleep or in a higher plane through meditation, that gravitational pull and bond to Earth is lessened allowing your soul and spirit to fly free once more—back to the Universal energy from which it came, back into the outstretched wings of God."*

When you are unconscious through sleep or in a higher plane through meditation, that gravitational pull and bond to Earth is lessened allowing your soul and spirit to fly free once more—back to the Universal energy from which it came, back into the outstretched wings of God. Let that freedom take flight and allow the pains and drains of earthly life to be released into the vast expanse of the Universe, sucked into a vortex or black hole, never to reappear again.

> *"Call upon the Universal energy of God to clear your soul and wipe clean the negative forces and lessons... lifting you to where you need to be in order to accomplish your true being's purpose."*

You must make the effort to release the burdens of your mind and your time-trapped earthly woes in order to be lifted above the mind-numbing pains that keep you knotted and rooted to past mistakes, strife and judgment. Call upon the Universal energy of God to clear your soul and wipe clean the negative forces and lessons which all lead to one simple conclusion—that you are centered in God and must release yourself from all that clings and claws at your soul, spiraling you in a downward crash and crippling fall of human struggle and strife. Once released of these burdens through conscious effort and through trust in the vast Universal goodness and wisdom, you will be ever-clear and light of heart and soul, mind and body. This frees you from the earthly pull and bonds, lifting you to where you need to be in order to accomplish your true being's purpose.

The vast knowledge of Universal energy is available for your use at every single moment in time. Call upon this power and ability to clear your mind and free your soul. Look to the heavens and take in this vast beauty and wonder. Feel the power and unlimited potential that creates and breathes life into your very being. Nothing is greater and nothing else resonates as does the wisdom of this Universal goodness, power and energy of God.

Allow the rays of the Sun to warm your heart and soothe your soul. Allow them to nurture and heal just as the Moon lulls you to rest in slumber

> *"Take in this energy—into the core of your being—and healing will be expedited and troubles dissolved, pains will be released and blocks cleared."*

Universal Energy

beneath the night sky. These two opposites have the same effect—acting in harmony to balance out the Earth and its inhabitants' discord. Take in this energy—into the core of your being—and healing will be expedited and troubles dissolved, pains will be released and blocks cleared.

> *"You are all One and all encompass the same energy. You must learn to go with the flow and stop resisting the truths-be-told and each other— fighting against the very essence of your being."*

The powers-that-be lie within the all-encompassing Universe and also lie within the center of you. Just as an atom lies at the center of your self within every cell of your being, so too do you lie within the center of the Universe itself within the core of your being. Everything is made up of the Universe and the Universe is made up of everything. You are all One and all encompass the same energy. You must learn to go with the flow and stop resisting the truths-be-told and each other—fighting against the very essence of your being.

Feel a part of the Universe—know that the vast wisdom and intelligence that creates and expands is also what creates and expands within you. Feel the surge of that power and rise above the limitations that your mind places upon your self and your own wisdom. The Universe along with its godly wisdom and power reside within the heart. Open up to this wisdom and you will open up your world to a whole new Light—a Light of being that creates and breathes life into all that is. You will open up to God Himself and become One with Him, living and breathing His Universal power, energy and Light.

> *"The Universe along with its godly wisdom and power reside within the heart."*

> *"Trust in this power and feel its presence in the experience of nature...Lift your arms to the sky and take this energy and Light into your heart and into the essence of your soul."*

Trust in this power and feel its presence in the experience of nature. Feel the power and energy of the Sun and the call of the Moon. Lift your arms to the sky and take this energy and Light into your heart and into the essence of your soul. Lift yourself above the pull and drain that humans must overcome—and experience a life of wonder and revelation. You have the choice—live consciously in each and every moment of your time on Earth. Transform your being, as well as that of humankind, through understanding and utilization of the Universal energy and power of God. All is good and all is just in the Light of God—all of which lives through the heart and not the mind—working toward harmony in a peaceful healing energy.

When negativity and judgment enter, this signifies that the Universal energy is being blocked. A conscious effort must then be made to shift and center yourself within your heart and focus upon bringing in the Light of God. Lift your eyes and arms to the sky to encompass the power and energy of the Sun and Moon, and experience the vast enlightenment and lifting that your soul needs for transformation. Call upon that God-given power and do your part to shine the Light of God in Universal truth and justice.

> *"When negativity and judgment enter, this signifies that the Universal energy is being blocked. A conscious effort must then be made to shift and center yourself..."*

♡

> *"Nature frees the soul from the traps of the mind,*
> *releasing it and centering it into the consciousness of the heart.*
> *It lifts the burdens of time and centers the vision*
> *into the beauty of the world—*
> *bringing life into the moment and to the present journey."*

 *November 25, 2009 (48 minutes)*

Nature: God's Glory

I shall now speak to you of nature and the beauty that gives rise to life. With the dawning of each new day arises the brightness and Light that springs forth from God's love and energy. It bathes the Earth in warmth and joy, sparkling with freshness that awakens the energy of life within. Watch as it washes over the Earth, beckoning to the buds to open toward the Light. Watch as it lifts the heads of the birds as they chirp and sing their way into the brightness of day. Watch as the waters of the streams glisten with the beauty of God's reflection. All are miracles sprung forth from the rising Sun. All are miracles that God has set before you, before mankind, to lift your hearts and the burdens of your minds, enabling heart-felt wisdom to spring forth—awakened through the beauty of nature.

Nature appeases the soul and launches the spirit. It quiets the mind and puts discontent to rest. It washes away worries and burdens from the past; and it nurtures life and the vision of God within. It pulls at the heartstrings and launches dreams. It dissolves blocks and whittles away pain. Nature is a gift from God, a gift to all life, and an embodiment of creation. It is an artistry of Light and beauty, wonder and awe. It sustains life and it reflects life, nurtures life and completes life.

> *"Nature and its beauty are crucial to the Light of the soul, providing the nourishment necessary to sustain the buoyancy of the spirit."*

Nature and its beauty are crucial to the Light of the soul, providing the nourishment necessary to sustain the buoyancy of the spirit. Through nature, man's spirit can be lifted and transcended by the power of God—heightened to a level of awareness so as to see its own beauty in the reflection of God's magnificence. Nature supplies the oxygen to its purpose and the lift to its flight. It is the wind that blows beneath the spirit's wings, launching it forth onto its journey to discover its heightened purpose and ability to fly. Nature frees the soul from the traps of the mind, releasing it and centering it into the consciousness of the heart. It lifts the burdens of time and centers the vision into the beauty of the world—bringing life into the moment and to the present journey.

> *"Nature is a reprieve, an escape from the hum-drum realities that settle into the man-created mechanized version of life. It brings man back to his roots... enabling him to rediscover what is truly meant to be."*

Nature is a reprieve, an escape from the hum-drum realities that settle into the man-created mechanized version of life. It brings man back to his roots, anchoring him in true reality enabling him to rediscover what is truly meant to be. It nurtures the heart and soul of the world, uniting all in a Oneness that can be shared and experienced by all—no matter how different the cultures, or thought patterns, or beliefs may be. It is true reality and true life, true gratitude and true nurturing of being. Nature encompasses all there is—all that is created out of love and Light and joy.

Nature: God's Glory

> *"Nature is self-regulating and flows with ease—
> nurturing and repairing, growing and seeding
> in a sustainment that is self-serving and self-creating,
> yet all-supporting and all-providing."*

Nature is self-regulating and flows with ease—nurturing and repairing, growing and seeding in a sustainment that is self-serving and self-creating, yet all-supporting and all-providing. It gives and receives without effort and in total harmony, balancing out all of Earth and its inhabitants. It provides for itself, yet its components feed off each other. It gives back, yet takes away—but only that which is necessary and beneficial for the survival of the whole. Nature is a pure example of how all should function—all of life, all that lives and breathes, all of humanity. It exemplifies how life should be—lived in wonder and awe, balanced in perfect harmony, flowing with God's Light and love of being.

Nature harmonizes for the good of the whole and the balance of the seasons. It comes and goes, ebbs and flows, showers and grows, nurtures and sows. It weeds and seeds, waters and feeds, laughs and cries, lives and dies. Nature lives and breathes life into the world and sprouts growth from the Earth and all of its inhabitants.

It provides all that is necessary to nurture the body and feed the soul, freeing mankind from the pressures of life when God's glory is experienced as it should be—when it is relished and enjoyed. One must free his time in order to experience the beauty in nature and in order to free his soul, enabling it to soar and be lifted to the level of God.

> *"One must free his time in order to experience the beauty
> in nature and in order to free his soul,
> enabling it to soar and be lifted to the level of God."*

> *"In order to sustain life, love and Light must be allowed to nurture the being within. Nature provides a vehicle for this..."*

God must be allowed to enter through the heart which is where love resides and life prevails. In order to sustain life, love and Light must be allowed to nurture the being within. Nature provides a vehicle for this to come about. It enables the mind to shut off its needless chatterings and open up to the beauty, wonder, and awe that encompasses the Earth—giving rise to life itself.

Within nature can be seen love and creation, painted with a palette of endless bounty from strokes colored with brilliance and imagination. Mankind must allow this life blood to flow through his veins, nurturing and sustaining the life of spirit within. For through nature, God's magnificence, power and wisdom are revealed—providing the answers to all of man's questions. Look to nature for the answers that you seek and for the peace of mind that is necessary to enable your soul to soar.

> *"Your mind will settle and your body will relax into a meditative state that nurtures and heals, releasing blocks and pains of the past. You will enable yourself to prepare for growth and opportunity..."*

Nature enters through the heart and provides wisdom to your being, lifting your life to where God intends it to be. Launch your life through opening your heart to God's magnificence and glory, which can be experienced through His ultimate brilliance—nature. Your mind will settle and your body will relax into a meditative state that nurtures and heals, releasing blocks and pains of the past. You will enable yourself to prepare for growth and opportunity through the release that nature provides and the nurturing that it offers.

Nature: God's Glory

God intends and desires good and glory for all. He has created all to sustain itself and to live in perfect harmony, but mankind must not fight against and destroy what God has created and provided. God intends that His gifts be cherished and utilized; those gifts are evident in nature and are boundless. Look to nature for the answers, for the peace, for the providing. That is where God lives and breathes in a glorious presentation that evidences His existence.

"Look to nature for the answers, for the peace, for the providing. That is where God lives and breathes in a glorious presentation that evidences His existence."

Section V
Tools for Transformation & Creation

Better to spread your wings and teach yourself how to fly,

than to wait around to be pushed off a cliff

into the great unknown.

"Look to nature and you will see God."

August 20, 2009 (42 minutes)

Nature's Healing Essence

Let us explore how the beauty of nature can transform mankind, lifting him out of his earthly pain and seesaw of torment and trouble. You have a purpose in this life and you must release your burdens and let your spirit soar, for the Lightness-of-being is ever present when you allow it to be. Free your soul and lift your spirits—all is not as helpless as it seems, all lies within the hands of God. Do not keep yourself down, burdened by the earthly pull that grabs at your troubled mind.

"Release your worries to the wind and let them blow clear of your being, clear of your essence—for they are not you and they must not anchor your spirit."

Release your worries to the wind and let them blow clear of your being, clear of your essence—for they are not you and they must not anchor your spirit. Allow your troubles to wash away with the tide, letting the waters clear the debris from your mind, burying the burdens that weigh you down. Release the pains of the past and look ahead into the distance. Watch the rising Sun and marvel at the force that created it, for He is the power and He is the love that can free you from all of your burdens.

See with vision the glory that God creates in His palette of magnificent colors. Watch in wonder as each day unfolds, springing forth an abundance of Light that lifts mankind—giving rise to his soul. Connect with

> *"...in the beauty of God's glory...reside the peace and tranquility of the now—that moment of time that stands still and stands alone from all else."*

this magnificence and help free your soul, opening to the glory that sparks within. Reach forth and discover the calling that resides within you all, beckoning you to nurture and cherish the gifts of nature.

Unlock the mysteries within your soul when you sit in the beauty of God's glory, for in this glory reside the peace and tranquility of the now—that moment of time that stands still and stands alone from all else. In the awe of God is released the worry and strife brought about by man's dwelling and toiling. There is nothing that can compare to what God creates. Within nature resides beauty, strength, courage, change, color and diversity—woven together by threads of natural wonder and inspiration.

Treasure the beauty and power that encompasses the Earth and is there for all to cherish. Take notice and clear your mind. Drink in this beauty and let it seep into your soul—healing and quieting the discontent that lies within. Watch for the signs from God, the evidence of His presence. There is nothing more glorious and incredible than the magnitude and multitude of His creations. What more does one need to evidence that there is a greater God or Creator? How can there not be?

Look to the heavens. Watch the changing sky as time stands still and floats by, drifting with the ever-changing formation of clouds. Revel in

> *"...in nature you touch God—reconnecting to your purpose and joy. Let this connection take place, and release the hurry and scurry of your world."*

this glory of artistry and Light. Let it wash over you and soothe and restore the callings of your soul, for in nature you touch God—reconnecting to your purpose and joy. Let this connection take place, and release the hurry and scurry of your world. Rise with the Sun and glow with the Moon. Sway with the trees and feel the whisper of the breeze.

Launch your spirit and your life's purpose through the calling of nature and the glory of God. Let go of the constraints and worries that life has placed upon you, and escape into the true realities of life, the true purpose for living, the essence of All That Is—that is God and creation, and is evidenced in nature. Sink back to your grass roots and feel the pull of the Earth and the beckoning of life. Let it seep into your soul and clear the fog from your head. Listen to the whispers of your heart and free your spirit, allowing it to take flight and lift the burdens of your mind.

> *"...within the true expression of nature...is where Heaven lies and where freedom flies. That is where God meets up with life and where life greets you with joy."*

> *"Nature...can release burdens in an instant— leaving you in awe and wonder with the realization that there is a God and He is always at your side, able to provide and protect, nurture and exonerate."*

All can be released by living in the moment, within the true expression of nature—that which seeps into your being and anchors your soul. That is where Heaven lies and where freedom flies. That is where God meets up with life and where life greets you with joy. Joy is the purpose of life and you must release your burdens in order to experience life as it should be. Nature provides this reprieve and can release burdens in an instant—leaving you in awe and wonder with the realization that there is a God and He is always at your side, able to provide and protect, nurture and exonerate.

"The more that you experience nature, the easier it is to live in the moment with conscious appreciation and gratitude for life and being. With gratitude comes release, and through release comes freedom and the clearing that is necessary to bring about change and abundance, love and Light."

Center yourself through nature and release your self-created humanly burdens. The more that you experience nature, the easier it is to live in the moment with conscious appreciation and gratitude for life and being. With gratitude comes release, and through release comes freedom and the clearing that is necessary to bring about change and abundance, love and Light. Nature is a touch of Heaven on Earth, and is clearly seen as so, when you take the time to truly appreciate its magnificence and beauty, wonder and enlightenment. Look to nature and you will see God.

"Joy is the purpose of life and you must release your burdens in order to experience life as it should be."

> *"God is the all-powerful, all-knowing glory of all creation...*
> *His energy emits forth in a nurturing, healing,*
> *protective Light...expanding and expounding, rebuilding and*
> *fortifying in a clear energy that dissipates the negative."*

 *February 4, 2010 (32 minutes)*

Prayer

God is the all-powerful, all-knowing glory of all creation—lit in spirit out of love and Light, encompassing the vastness of the Universe. His energy emits forth in a nurturing, healing, protective Light that answers to the prayers of all His children—expanding and expounding, rebuilding and fortifying in a clear energy that dissipates the negative.

Prayer is a vehicle for communication with God. It is the asking for a desired gift of Light through faith and appreciation for the greater power that resides beyond the human self. Prayer is offered through conscious effort out of hope in a giving of trust to the greater powers-that-be. With prayer you make this conscious desire known to God and angelic beings, as well as to your higher-self, in a faithful request for the achievement of well-being for yourself or for others. You ask in expectation of receiving,

> *"Prayer is a vehicle for communication with God.*
> *It is the asking for a desired gift of Light*
> *through faith and appreciation for*
> *the greater power that resides beyond the human self."*

> *"...subconscious chatter can be detrimental as it manifests and brings about undesired effects in a whirlwind of creation spun out of dislocated and unintended thoughts."*

of being granted this wish that is set forth into the Universal energy and expansive power of Light—the Light of God. This is the traditional mode of prayer.

Prayer expands much beyond this, for it is also created out of expectation and repetitive patterns of thought brought about by the mind's incessant chatter. This subconscious chatter can be detrimental as it manifests and brings about undesired effects in a whirlwind of creation spun out of dislocated and unintended thoughts. To avoid this detrimental trap, it is crucial to gain control over your thoughts and their resulting feelings which are created from an overruling mind. In order to accomplish this and quiet and contain the mind, you must learn to control the mind through heartfelt focus and wisdom—unleashing the true power and connection of your being to the Almighty God.

> *"Once your thoughts are reined in and the heart gains control, manifestation as to what you truly desire unfolds, lifting your spirit and expanding your world to encompass godly creation, wisdom and Light."*

Once your thoughts are reined in and the heart gains control, manifestation as to what you truly desire unfolds, lifting your spirit and expanding your world to encompass godly creation, wisdom and Light. When this power of knowing and self-control is achieved, you are able to much more effectively pray and receive the answers, wisdom, and creation in an all-knowing Light of truth and manifestation. You gain control over your intentional prayers, obtaining confidence in the acquiring of the desired results; and you relinquish and dissolve the unintentional "prayers" of your dislocated thoughts and unintended focus which often bring about the exact opposite of what you truly desire—for your mind's focus when not reined in tends to gravitate toward the negative with worry over what you do NOT want to transpire.

> *"God...orchestrates into being and coordinates through magnificence and wonder a Master Plan that answers the prayers of all in a way that nurtures the callings of each individual's higher-self."*

Prayer is the asking of God. Once this is done, you must let go and trust that God will provide the best vehicle or mode for delivering your request. Sometimes the resulting mode is not what you may have intended or through the means that you may have expected, but God has greater wisdom and broader vision than any one man can see. He has all-knowing wisdom and power that expands even beyond the Universe—a knowing so great that He can see all and all the facets of any given situation. He orchestrates into being and coordinates through magnificence and wonder a Master Plan that answers the prayers of all in a way that nurtures the callings of each individual's higher-self.

You must trust that things are being orchestrated as they should. Be patient and allow for the wisdom of God to show its face, revealing itself when the time is right and the results are maximized for planned-out learning and benefit to the multiple parties involved—for you are all

> *"Trust is key and release is crucial, knowing that God has the true wisdom and means of achieving the desired results that benefit His children."*

vehicles for each other's growth and are orchestrated into each other's lives for purposes that are sometimes not visible to the human eye. There is a much greater plan involved that encompasses multiple levels of being and consciousness—expanding and growing into the generations to come for the transformation of the entire destiny of mankind. Trust is key and release is crucial, knowing that God has the true wisdom and means of achieving the desired results that benefit His children.

You must learn to tap in to the wisdom of your heart, for the heart can feel the essence of the Creator and His wisdom that springs forth. The heart is what taps in to the miracles and beauty of the Universe—the miracles of God. The strongest prayers are those that come from the heart in selfless desire, projected out of love and Light. Those are the ones that carry the greatest power and are answered by God in the purest form—encompassing and spreading His Light to benefit not only the soul that is the focus of the request, but also the requester himself, for to live through God in selfless giving of the heart is the greatest gift of all and achieves what God intends for all of mankind.

"God's Master Plan includes the transformation of mankind into beings of Light that are a true reflection of God Himself—living out of love and Light through the heart in a nurturing exchange of selfless giving that answers the prayers of each other."

God's Master Plan includes the transformation of mankind into beings of Light that are a true reflection of God Himself—living out of love and Light through the heart in a nurturing exchange of selfless giving that answers the prayers of each other. Once that is achieved, there will be no lack or greed, struggle or strife, and the Earth will become a paradise of pure love, creation and being—residing out of fairness, truth and justice for all in a harmonious song of the heart and a magical, magnificent dance of Light.

> *"Pray for the ability to open up to the Light of God and for the enabling of your heart and soul to tune in to that love and Light...That is the ultimate prayer... as you will all learn to live through God and of-God..."*

Pray for the ability to open up to the Light of God and for the enabling of your heart and soul to tune in to that love and Light. Trust in the knowing that the answers will be provided and the lessons manifested in order to bring about your highest good for the transformation of your soul and the souls of mankind in order to create a true paradise and Heaven on Earth. That is the ultimate prayer and the one that will bring this reality into being as you will all learn to live through God and of-God, answering your own prayers as you will be lifted to the level of God Himself.

Trust that you are being guided and trust that you are being listened to, reining in your mind and detrimental thoughts. Let go, knowing that there is a wisdom and presence that is much more expansive, all-knowing and powerful than any other energy or power that exists—creating and orchestrating events and circumstances, relationships and manifestations in a Master Plan of forthcoming achievement that answers to the greater-good of creation and life itself.

> *"Let go, knowing that there is a wisdom and presence that is much more expansive, all-knowing and powerful than any other...creating and orchestrating... in a Master Plan of forthcoming achievement that answers to the greater-good of creation and life itself."*

Visual Prayer of Protection:

I live in a house of crystal filled with Light.
No darkness shall enter but for the sky of night.
My vision has no limits, my being no bounds.
God is my protector whose energy surrounds.

"Sleep redefines the soul's purpose & sets the course for action."

 *August 12, 2009 (41 minutes)*

Sleep

Sleep is a mystery to mankind. Sleep redefines the soul's purpose and sets the course for action. It defies the mind and creates a mystery with man's concept of time. When you let go and relax your mind, you float off into space, a realm that lies beyond the mind—one which is not trapped within the bounds of human thought pattern. Here in this state you transcend into a mix of subconscious patterns of thought and flickerings of the soul's scatterings and realities. The mind translates these as "dreams" rather than alter-existences and experiences.

"Sleep helps to heal the soul from the discontent of the human conscious experience. It intermingles the mind with the eye of God, enabling super-intelligence and healing..."

Sleep helps to heal the soul from the discontent of the human conscious experience. It intermingles the mind with the eye of God, enabling super-intelligence and healing to take its course. You drift in and out of dream states in order to allow your mind to filter an awareness and intelligence that is beyond the human grasp. This intelligence, this nurturing, this rest from strife and conscious struggle, soothe and nurture the soul enabling it to renew and restructure in order to move forth along the hard and rocky human path. This rest, this renewal, is essential in order to complete the journey—as it is an exhausting one.

 Like an uphill climb for a mountaineer, breaks must be taken and equipment mended or he will be ill-prepared for an avalanche. His footing must be sure and his cleats sharp in order to get a grip on "reality", or simply the surface of the mountain he climbs. That mountainous terrain is a hard road to tow and if exhaustion sets in, the journey becomes impossible. The path is much brighter and is clearer to see with the dawning of a new day, just as life's trials and tribulations are much easier to take when given a fresh start and a new more visible direction—as is accomplished through sleep.

> *"Watch for the clues within your dreams, the fears that you must face and the lessons that your life path weaves forth. Discover who you are and who you are being called into becoming..."*

With sleep comes guidance into your deepest concerns and problems that are currently afoot. Also forthcoming are lessons that must be learned and messages sent from God. Dive into these messages and look at the deeper meaning, those meanings that only you can translate from your own personal experiences and knowledge. That is where the answers lie—the hints at what must be revealed in order to solve your personal mysteries and set you on the path to growth and discovery. Watch for the clues within your dreams, the fears that you must face and the lessons that your life path weaves forth. Discover who you are and who you are being called into becoming from your dreams and the whisperings of the night.

> *"Within the sleep state you are defined and examined, taught and nurtured, inspired and directed. You connect with different realms and different existences."*

> *"...there are hidden messages and meanings within each dream's story."*

When you are at peace in a restful state, your subconscious opens to the wisdom from Above and from within your very being, your very soul. Take heart and "listen" with an open mind, one that reaches beyond traditional human thinking—for the messages unravel in riddles. Look deep within your spirit to discover your true purpose and calling. Within the sleep state you are defined and examined, taught and nurtured, inspired and directed. You connect with different realms and different existences. Your human mind has trouble deciphering this and works the translations into riddles that play tricks on the mind. Unravel the riddles and solve the puzzle, for there are hidden messages and meanings within each dream's story.

With sleep you open up to God's wisdom and teachings. You enter a state that is susceptible and amiable, one that is able to more readily receive a higher vibration and, therefore, a stronger signal that can alter the patterns of the brain creating a transformation and development of changed thinking. Through this changed thinking the soul can step forward more readily and easily onto its destined path. The nurturing of the mind, body and spirit during the sleep state is unsurpassed by any other state, other than meditation. Meditation differs in that you remain fully conscious so that thought can be directed and healing can be accelerated.

> *"You enter a state that is susceptible and amiable, one that is able to more readily receive a higher vibration and, therefore, a stronger signal that can alter the patterns of the brain creating a transformation and development of changed thinking."*

> *"Meditation is an all-important and crucial means of spiritual peace that must be practiced...in order to foster an inner awareness and connection with the outer greatness of God and the Universal energy that springs forth."*

 *November 7, 2009 (48 minutes)*

Meditation

Meditation is an all-important and crucial means of spiritual peace that must be practiced by humankind in order to foster an inner awareness and connection with the outer greatness of God and the Universal energy that springs forth. Watch your soul's transformation as you tap into the mind's eye and relax into the peace of the Universe. You float off into space, releasing the earthly burdens and gravitational pull that strains your mind and drains your spirit.

> *"You turn off and tune out your mind, and turn on and tune in to your heart connection and vision through your all-seeing mind's eye."*

With meditation you connect with your inner knowing and guidance that can bring forth peace of mind, body and spirit. This is done through concentration to release thought. You turn off and tune out your mind, and turn on and tune in to your heart connection and vision through your all-seeing mind's eye. Your pattern of thought must be released and let go, through either visualization and the bringing in of Light, or through the simple repetition of a word or phrase, or through concentration on breathing. There are limitless methods, but the ultimate purpose is to block out the mind's thinking in order to open up to the vast expanse of Universal knowledge and connection which lies beyond the mind.

> *"Meditation clears the energy fields, and filters and cleanses your being. It allows information to enter that is from a higher plane and greater wisdom."*

When the mind is not turned off or set aside, it clutters your being—creating a static that blocks out the higher vibration and energy which can be received through meditation. Meditation clears the energy fields, and filters and cleanses your being. It allows information to enter that is from a higher plane and greater wisdom. It brings forth Light, the Light of God, into your soul and being in order to heal, cleanse and soothe—bringing peace to your path and to your life. You reach a higher vibration and frequency that is rarely achieved during your human waking-hours. This gives you reprieve from the pressures and drains of life, which take their toll on your being.

Healing is expedited, and once meditation with focus and guided direction is mastered, the healing results are unsurpassed. You gain control over your entire being, its health, direction and purpose. You are able to filter in information that is for your highest good, directed from God the Almighty. You achieve Universal connection and merge with this energy, becoming renewed and lifted in spirit. Meditation is a marvel and a must—a method to achieve power-of-being and renewal, and to acquire energy and Light. With practice renewal, nurturing and healing can be instantaneous.

> *"Meditation is...a method to achieve power-of-being and renewal, and to acquire energy and Light."*

One must sit in quiet. Focus, and direct the mind into peace with whatever method is chosen. Say a short prayer of protection, directing the Light of God into and surrounding your being. Center your vision inward into your mind's eye, and shift your consciousness away from your mind and into your heart. Relax and focus. Once you achieve a state of peace, you are then able to merge with the energy of the Universe—the energy of God—to lift your burdens and your health. Your being will radiate with the Light of God, enabling patterns of thought to be altered, healed and mended in this state.

> *"You will enable the mastering of your own health as you direct healing Light and energy forth, clearing away blocks and pains."*

You will be lifted to the level of God's wonder and will acquire wisdom and answers to unanswered questions. You will be nudged toward your destined path, and your soul will be fed and nourished. The mind's eye will see what the human eyes are unable to see—into the Great Beyond with vision and clarity; and the heart will hear the whisperings of God and angelic guidance. You will enable the mastering of your own health as you direct healing Light and energy forth, clearing away blocks and pains.

Meditation is a method of transformation and enlightenment that must be mastered through practice and patience. Patience is a virtue and the process cannot be rushed or stressed, as the whole purpose and technique is peace—peace within itself. You will achieve peace out of peace, in a

> *"You will achieve peace out of peace, in a looping effect that expands with time and practice—enabling your being to achieve perfect balance and harmony within itself."*

Meditation

looping effect that expands with time and practice—enabling your being to achieve perfect balance and harmony within itself. When you are in harmony and at peace, your body resonates with the vibration of God, your path brightens, and your vision and truth come into focus. Peace is the key and meditation achieves that.

Practice the technique of meditation on a consistent basis, just as you eat and sleep on a consistent basis. When you do so, your life flows more easily with less struggle and discord, your health maintains balance, and your relationships blossom. You bring yourself into a higher level of being and are better able to withstand the pressures of life.

---

*"Mediation can be used to direct self-healing,
achieve relaxation and stress release,
maintain or achieve balance, achieve higher vibration levels,
receive guidance, insight or wisdom,
and direct healing energy or messages to others."*

Meditation brings about the same benefits of sleep, but due to the level of consciously-guided focus, you are able to direct with purpose and determination—achieving and accomplishing that which you consciously set out to achieve. Mediation can be used to direct self-healing, achieve relaxation and stress release, maintain or achieve balance, achieve higher vibration levels, receive guidance, insight or wisdom, and direct healing energy or messages to others.

Meditation is a guidepost for your life—giving you direction, peace of mind and reprieve as you travel along your journey. It enables you to achieve balance and live in perfect harmony with yourself, understanding the truth of your being. Meditation puts you in a relaxation state that drains away the stressors and pressures of life, enabling your life to flow with ease and less resistance.

> *"This state of consciousness is unsurpassed in its vibrational level...transforming your life forth onto the path that you are meant to travel."*

This state of consciousness is unsurpassed in its vibrational level, enabling the wisdom of God and the truth-of-being to flow into your mind's eye and through your heart, transforming your life forth onto the path that you are meant to travel. You enable yourself to tune in to God's wisdom, decipher its meaning, and distinguish that wisdom from your own mental, misguided chatterings—laying to rest the burdens that your mind and the earthly pull of life place upon your soul which anchor your spirit from its flight of freedom. Let go and let your spirit soar, lifting the vibration of your being and your life, through meditation.

> *"You enable yourself to tune in to God's wisdom, decipher its meaning, and distinguish that wisdom from your own mental, misguided chatterings— laying to rest the burdens... which anchor your spirit from its flight of freedom."*

> *"The mind's eye lies at the center of your inner vision—
> your seeing into the creation and the Creator, His purpose,
> and His callings and teachings."*

 *August 9, 2009 (24 minutes)*

The Mind's Eye

Seek not the answers elsewhere, for the wisdom lies within your own soul and at the heart of your roots—those roots that intertwine with the Earth and its realities in space and time. Leap ahead into your mind's eye in order to see and clarify your vision—that is where the true answers dwell. The mind's eye lies at the center of your inner vision—your seeing into the creation and the Creator, His purpose, and His callings and teachings. Reach forth and seek the wisdom and answers here.

> *"This is a place that dwells deep within the peaceful
> presence of your being combining with the whisperings of
> God's truths. The mind's eye houses the answers
> that lie buried beneath the burdens of the human mind."*

This is a place that dwells deep within the peaceful presence of your being combining with the whisperings of God's truths. The mind's eye houses the answers that lie buried beneath the burdens of the human mind. Stretch forth to see what lies within and beyond in this vast expanse of peaceful wisdom and all-knowing, for the blessings are revealed once you enter through this porthole or gate of knowledge

> *"To enter into this vision, you must keep clear of thought and your mind's prodding and simply look deep within, 'listening' for the answers and seeking the visions that come forth."*

and Light. That is the eye to the mind, unlocking its mysteries and the mysteries of the Universe—and it is the window into your soul.

To enter into this vision, you must keep clear of thought and your mind's prodding and simply look deep within, "listening" for the answers and seeking the visions that come forth. Untrap your soul and light the inner fire that kindles, until it blossoms with the flame of God's Light and love. That is how you come into knowing and open up to the wisdom within the mind's eye—an everlasting source of abundance and a wealth of knowledge and love, centered through God Himself.

> *"...sit in peace and in quiet, clearing your mind and shifting your consciousness to your heart. This will clear the way and allow the mind's eye to open... in will enter the messages that you seek deep within your soul—answers that spark with the infinite wisdom of God."*

Let go of the mind blocks that you have created and sit in peace and in quiet, clearing your mind and shifting your consciousness to your heart. This will clear the way and allow the mind's eye to open. Once open, in will enter the messages that you seek deep within your soul—answers that spark with the infinite wisdom of God. Pray for your highest good and for the highest good of mankind, wrapping yourself with love and Light and you shall be protected by God Himself, for God resides in all and is there to protect and offer peace spreading abundance and love throughout His Kingdom. The mind's eye is the way in which this Universal wisdom enters into the human spirit or soul.

Cherish this peaceful presence, this porthole of inner space, and seek within for the peace and comfort, the knowing and guidance that can enter forth into your being. There is a wealth of wisdom and an infinite amount of guidance that is available once you open up the mind's eye. Unveil this wonder and discover what awaits to reveal the truths that are all within your sight and all within your reach.

Set forth to discover all that there is to see with ease and unrestraint. Lift your spirits to the heavens and take flight into this wondrous journey of discovery and knowledge, wisdom and insight—one that supersedes all others. You become a diamond in the sky twinkling with the heavens, when you allow yourself to absorb and reflect the Light of God. The mind's eye is the quickest, most direct way to let this Light enter into your being, making you a beacon for the transmission of messages through and from God Himself. Allow these messages to filter through and come forth and you will awaken the truths that stir within your soul, lighting the power within and showing the way for you and others to follow—for you are all creatures of God, created in His image, created for the purpose of spreading His Light. You are not meant to suffer, but simply to learn how to live and how to love and how to shine the Light of God, transforming the world at hand.

Shine forth, my child of God. Let God Himself merge into the knowing that lies within—a knowing that simply needs to be sparked and ignited in order to come into being.

"You are not meant to suffer, but simply to learn how to live and how to love and how to shine the Light of God, transforming the world at hand."

 *December 1, 2009 (44 minutes)*

Body Movement & Nourishment

Now I shall speak to you of what humans consider to be exercise but shall refer to it simply as body movement. Body movement is necessary in order to clear and release the energy blocks that get trapped within the body and energy field of your being. These blocks settle in and get lodged, needing to be freed through either physical movement, or mental and spiritual focus, or a combination of the two. Some forms of exercise combine both means of release, achieving end-results at an expedited pace. Whatever the form, physical movement must take place in order to achieve proper functioning of the body, enabling blocks to be dissolved and healing energy to flow.

> *"You must release the discomforts and dis-ease, as they can cripple the body and hamper the spirit in an endless cycle of debilitating loss of self— draining the life that flows through you."*

The flow of life through the blood stream is crucial in order to wash away the pains of life and distress that settles into your body and being. You must release the discomforts and dis-ease, as they can cripple the body and hamper the spirit in an endless cycle of debilitating loss of self—draining the life that flows through you. When you feel discomfort, tension or pain, that is your body's signal that there is a kink in your life needing to be worked out. This may reside purely in the physical— perhaps acquired through repetitive strain or trauma; or this may simply have settled in the physical, building up as a result of discontent within

> *"Physical movement...improves the blood flow—the flow of life's energy—throughout the body, helping to disperse the negative energy blocks that settle within."*

the spiritual realm of being—perhaps due to an ignoring by the mind of an issue that nags discontent within the heart or spirit-of-being.

Physical movement, or exercise, helps to clear these blocks within the body and can also clear the mind. It improves the blood flow—the flow of life's energy—throughout the body, helping to disperse the negative energy blocks that settle within. It gives the mind reprieve and calms the chatterings, as the mind's energy is redirected and utilized to focus on the physical activity at-hand, enabling healing energy to flow and soothe the mind itself.

> *"With exercise that utilizes visualization or mind focus... results are achieved at an unsurpassable speed. This is accomplished due to the meditative quality that relaxes the mind, enabling the Light of God to enter forth and offer its own healing Light in combination with the self-directed means."*

With exercise that utilizes visualization or mind focus, such as yoga, qigong, tai chi, or simply another form where thought is consciously directed to expedite healing, results are achieved at an unsurpassable speed. This is accomplished due to the meditative quality that relaxes the mind, enabling the Light of God to enter forth and offer its own healing Light in combination with the self-directed means. All can be accomplished through movement and focus, visualization and Light. The body can be realigned and brought into perfect balance, enabling you to move forth in your life and achieve what you are destined to and have set out to accomplish.

"When you limit your beliefs and ignore your own guidance signals, you limit yourself—creating blocks that manifest into pain and discomfort...you must work to release them before they cripple you up in a state of unrest, confusing you as to your own power-of-being and role in life creation."

When you limit your beliefs and ignore your own guidance signals, you limit yourself—creating blocks that manifest into pain and discomfort. With this, you must work to release them before they cripple you up in a state of unrest, confusing you as to your own power-of-being and role in life creation. Let go of the worry of the world and the constraints that pull and unrest your soul, twisting your body and tying it into knots that wreak havoc with your system. Through movement and focus you can begin to dissolve the distresses of life and the knots that you have tied yourself into, relinquishing the pains and stumbling blocks of the past—freeing yourself and your life and enabling the flight of your soul.

Work to knead out these knots and kinks of life, and offer yourself the opportunity for growth and new exploration by removing your troubled physical burdens from your list of detours and misguided stumbling blocks. Life is meant to flow with ease and joy, and life's energy is meant to flow, without restraint, through your body. Physical movement keeps the energy of life flowing, enabling a cascading of abundance and joy, freedom and energy to surge through your mind, body and spirit. This is the very essence of your life—the life that resides within your self—pumped by God and offered to you through Universal law and guiding Light. Let that energy flow freely, so as to not create your own blocks and pains. Seek to continue forth that flow of life, through movement and focus, in order to channel the healing Light and energy of God and the Universe.

Proper nutrition also plays a crucial role in the flow of life-energy through the blood stream. Certain foods such as sugar, chemicals and unhealthy fats will clog or weaken the body's resources, while others will nourish

> *"When your body feels sluggish or out of sorts with what you ingest, you are weighed and pulled down—hampering the wholeness of your being."*

and enrich the blood of life. Mind what you eat, and pay attention to your body's signals as to what provides the nourishment and energy that it needs to properly sustain and enhance the life within. When your body feels sluggish or out of sorts with what you ingest, you are weighed and pulled down—hampering the wholeness of your being.

Take responsibility for what you can control, with regard to your life and those lives that are under your care. It will make a world of difference by enabling and providing optimal body performance to that vehicle which houses the precious gift of life within—the soul of your being. Treasure that which you have been gifted and granted by God—a finely tuned machine-of-life that provides all that is necessary to offer protection and transportation to your spirit-of-being, enabling it to move freely forth and shine its presence and Light throughout the Earth. Through proper maintenance, your body aids in the task of your life's purpose—rather than inhibits your freedom and mobility—enabling you to accomplish your mission from God and gift to your inner being.

> *"Treasure that which you have been gifted and granted by God—a finely tuned machine-of-life that provides all that is necessary to offer protection and transportation to your spirit-of-being, enabling it to move freely forth and shine its presence and Light throughout the Earth."*

♡

> *"...health transforms as you allow God's healing to touch your very soul, washing through your being—cleansing and unblocking the barriers that you have created through your mind-blocks and self-imposed limitations."*

August 16, 2009 (51 minutes)

Healing

God is there to comfort and heal all those that truly ask for His assistance and seek well-being. He has the power to heal all—all ailments, all worries, all of the demons that lie within a tormented soul. He has the power above all else, if only asked, for He is there to nurture and to cherish, to love and to embrace—enfolding the world in peace and Light, joy and health. He is a wellspring of abundance and blessings offered to all in exchange for appreciation and servitude, gratitude and being.

Shed your Light upon those surrounding you and you will be lifted to the level of God, for God is love and God is gratitude, God is Light and God is wealth in cherished moments. Feel the peace and healing that is presented when God is allowed to enter through your heart and into your mind's eye, washing away the blocks and pains of mankind. Free your soul to this magnificence and miracle of the heart, as love knows no bounds and is inspired by the wisdom of the all-knowing God—the life force that resides in all. This limitless servitude is offered to all humankind and is there for the asking and there for the taking. It is your right and is held in high esteem awaiting your use. Simply open your mind and heart to this inner knowing and this outer magnificence of unearthly wisdom and greatness.

Watch as your health transforms as you allow God's healing to touch your very soul, washing through your being—cleansing and unblocking the barriers that you have created through your mind-blocks and self-imposed limitations. Free yourself from this bondage and awaken to the dawning of a new day—the discovery of that healing power within your own being that springs forth when you tap into your Creator and call upon the resources that have been granted unto you, His precious child, the one that reflects His love and inner Light of health and abundance.

> *"Transform your health through the knowingness that the power to do so lies within."*

> *"Heal the mind, body & soul, as the spirit has multiple levels that must be freed of the dis-ease that clings to your discontent."*

Seek the answers within your own heart, those that call to you from your deeper inner being. Transform your health through the knowingness that the power to do so lies within. Feel the surge of life force that can transform and heal, dissolve and conquer. Allow the Light of God to enter and cleanse the wounds that rip and shred at your soul's content. Clear the slate and wash it clean with liquid Light that seeps into your inner being. Heal the mind, body and soul, as the spirit has multiple levels that must be freed of the dis-ease that clings to your discontent.

Wash away the sorrow, and spring forth into a new tomorrow. Let go and release the pains of the past, knowing that a new day is dawning filled with brighter skies and clearer vision. God is always there to soothe and heal the wounds created from the past and anchored in the generations that brought them about. Let go of these chains and free yourself, allowing the Light of God to relinquish the pains and lift your soul and life to new glorious beginnings.

> *"You are never alone, never left to suffer as one."*

> *"...miracles happen every day. They can be set forth in a flick of an instant, a shift in thinking, a moment in time, a grant of a wish, or a change of mind."*

You are never alone, never left to suffer as one. God is always present and is always your peace—simply open up to that loving embrace and allow yourself to be sheltered by His love and protection. He will not let you down. He will lift your spirits and heal the damage that has been done. You simply must allow Him to do so. Open up the mind's eye and open up your heart in order to allow the healing to begin. It is never too late to begin the process—as miracles happen every day. They can be set forth in a flick of an instant, a shift in thinking, a moment in time, a grant of a wish, or a change of mind. Let those miracles in, allow them to unfold and wrap you in a blanket of loving, healing Light.

Feel the power within when you tap into that unyielding resource of all-knowing, all-conquering healing. Let it gel into reality, allowing the miracle of healing to rebirth the vitality of the life within your cells and your being. The ever-presence of God will wash away the pain and illness once you free yourself from your limited thinking and allow the transformation to take place. Direct this energy throughout your body, surging the life force—the Light energy of God—throughout your being, clearing the way and dissolving all blocks within its path. Direct this with your mind, with the vision of your mind's eye, and with the Light and energy from your heart. Hold this and push it forth with conviction and

> *"Focus & visualize clear health & Lightness of being, for the power lies within & throughout, merging at your heart center & illuminating outward, encompassing your being in ever-clear Light that revitalizes the cells & seeps into the soul."*

belief, trusting in the greatness of God—and all will be clear, all will be right, all will manifest, all will be bright.

Walk forward and do not get caught up in the past and those limitations that have dragged your spirit down. They weaken the soul's power and damage the spirit and body, warping the mind. Let go, release, and let God. Trust and believe. Focus and visualize clear health and Lightness of being, for the power lies within and throughout, merging at your heart center and illuminating outward, encompassing your being in ever-clear Light that revitalizes the cells and seeps into the soul.

Watch and learn, look and listen to the whisperings of discontent that lie within your body's pains. Relinquish these by dissolving the beliefs that are rooted within and intertwine, holding you back from the life that you are meant to live. Live gloriously and with freedom—freedom from the bondage of a limited mind that is trapped in disbelief of the power that is ever-present. Release the grip of your past and let go of the worry that traps you and trips you up, creating stumbling blocks that damage your health through discontent and disconnection from your life's purpose and inner being.

---

*"Live gloriously and with freedom—
freedom from the bondage of a limited mind that is trapped
in disbelief of the power that is ever-present."*

---

*"Release the grip of your past and let go of the worry
that traps you and trips you up, creating stumbling blocks
that damage your health through discontent and
disconnection from your life's purpose and inner being."*

 *December 1, 2009 (45 minutes)*

Inner Guidance

Let us take the topic of Inner guidance. The wisdom of God centers within your heart and resonates throughout your being. You must simply tune in, in order to receive these messages and distinguish them from the chatterings of your mind. This inner knowing is crucial to your well-being, for it alarms you when there is distress or danger present, alerts you when you are being misdirected, nudges you forth in the direction of your higher purpose and path, and signals you when you need to take action for your highest good. This is your radar—your gut response—and it is a necessity to your well-being.

"When you tune in to this guidance from God, you tune in to the opportunity for peace, love and trust. You let go of the mind-traps that nag discontent and that keep you from walking forth into future growth and enlightenment."

When you tune in to this guidance from God, you tune in to the opportunity for peace, love and trust. You let go of the mind-traps that nag discontent and that keep you from walking forth into future growth and enlightenment. God and angelic beings are at the helm of these signals—guiding and directing, nudging and prodding. Take heed and listen to these whisperings that offer true wisdom and guidance, rather than to the trickery that is played out by your mind.

Of course, the mind is a crucial tool for weighing out a decision. It is to be utilized to decipher and analyze, compare and contrast. It is necessary in order to calculate the rationality of a matter or the feasibility of a solution.

Inner Guidance

> *"Intuition and guidance come into play...when they wrestle in opposition to the mind. That is where you need to take note and side with your heart rather than your head."*

Intuition and guidance come into play and into the mix of things, when they wrestle in opposition to the mind. That is where you need to take note and side with your heart rather than your head. It is from the heart that truth and greater wisdom resonate—a signal pulling from the greater resources that sing to your soul or inner being, rather than from the workings of a twisting and turning mind.

> *"There is a reason for the signal, a necessity that answers a higher calling—one that you may be unaware of. Yet it exists and should be followed in order to fulfill that higher purpose for your self or for someone else's need."*

> *"Follow your gut and walk your own line—one that leads straight to the heart and into the arms of angelic guidance."*

When you feel discontent within, take heed and note the feeling and pull of your being. Listen to the signal and follow its cue. You will be glad you did, as you will not be steered wrong. There is a reason for the signal, a necessity that answers a higher calling—one that you may be unaware of. Yet it exists and should be followed in order to fulfill that higher purpose for your self or for someone else's need. Let go of your mind-traps and society-molded pressures. Do not go against the grain of your beliefs and the pull of your heartstrings in order to appease the expectations of others. Follow your gut and walk your own line—one that leads straight to the heart and into the arms of angelic guidance. What can be more all-knowing and truthful than the wisdom of God and the laws of the Universe?

You each have a purpose and you each must strive to reach that life-serving calling as quickly as possible. Through inner guidance and outer all-expansive wisdom, that can be accomplished much more quickly as God knows of your higher purpose—He knows all. Let His wisdom seep into your being and signal your heart. Tune in to the inner and outer signals that are boundless. These signals appear not only through nudgings felt within, but also through "coincidences" you experience throughout your day and your life. A simple chance encounter with a long-time friend, a coincidental avoidance of an accident, a finding of money just as it is needed—these are all miracles of life, messages of God signifying the Light and magic that abounds.

"Note these miracles and live with joy, knowing that you are always being guided, always being signaled. You simply need to tune in to hear or to feel or to notice the messages."

Note these miracles and live with joy, knowing that you are always being guided, always being signaled. You simply need to tune in to hear or to feel or to notice the messages. God is always at your side, offering help and assistance when needed, nudging you back onto the right path in order to avoid unnecessary hardship and pain. Once you tune in to your own inner guidance and the vast messages of the Universe, your life will flow with ease, lifting the burdens of doubt that creep into your mind.

"...the mind does not know the true, greater wisdom that can only be translated through the heart...It beats with the rhythm of God and feels discord when the energy does not balance in harmony with God's essence."

The pressure will be released, as your mind will no longer be held responsible for what it does not and is not capable of knowing—for the mind does not know the true, greater wisdom that can only be translated through the heart. The heart tunes in with a sensitivity that vibrates to the song of God, resonating with truth and wisdom, love and Light. It offers what no other organ of the human body can. It beats with the rhythm of God and feels discord when the energy does not balance in harmony with God's essence. The heart signals the body of this discord, and it is the brain's responsibility to respond and utilize the information that the heart passes along.

Keep your mind in check, and become aware of the signals that come through your heart and how they resonate with God's truth—enabling your being to relax into the wisdom of the All-Knowing. Through God's direction and perfect guidance, you can do no wrong. You simply must learn to follow this wisdom and tune in to the signals that you feel and which are set forth into your life. Your life will become much simpler to understand, and your decisions will become much easier to make.

Pray for guidance and direction, and the answers will follow. Look, listen and learn, to uncover the secrets of the heart and the wisdom that resonates forth. Through practice and in time, you will hone this skill and will be able to readily distinguish the messages of your heart from the chatterings of your mind. Your heart will become refined, and you will tune in to the dance of life and the melody of God's whisperings.

"Your heart will become refined, and you will tune in to the dance of life and the melody of God's whisperings."

> *"Within the heart lie the answers to all of life's mysteries and wonders—a knowing so great that only the eye of God can see farther."*

October 4, 2009 (33 minutes)

Wisdom of the Heart

The whispers of the heart tell a tale of magnificence and beauty beyond the visible, expanding your world to encompass the wisdom of God and the Light of the Universe—unleashing the power within and the shining glory that you are meant to become. Within the heart lie the answers to all of life's mysteries and wonders—a knowing so great that only the eye of God can see farther. The heart is where your soul meets and connects with this Source. Shine forth in all your glory, lifting your spirit on the wings of prayer to meet with the heavens above. Let your soul soar to unlimited heights, expanding with the vast Universe of knowledge, wisdom, and Light—merging and intermingling at the center of your being encompassing All That Is.

> *"The whispers of the heart tell a tale of magnificence and beauty beyond the visible...unleashing the power within and the shining glory that you are meant to become."*

Listen to the whispers that guide and direct, lift and offer love in an all-encompassing healing energy that soothes your soul and quiets your mind. You are all One and all can open to this magnificent Light of knowing—centered within the core of your being radiating through your heart. Shift your consciousness from your mind to your heart to feel this vast power

> *"The brain is simply a tool; the heart is your source—your source of wisdom, love, Light and Universal energy."*

> *"With focus and clarity, in will come the messages that will lift you, your life and mankind into a higher level of being—where the mind and heart are open and the soul is free."*

and energy within, for it resonates and speaks to the vibration of God. He is there to lift and guide, giving direction through your heart, as your heart tunes in to this energy.

Do not battle with your mind in a game of wits and war. Tune out your mind and settle deep within your soul, for the true wisdom lies there. The mind plays tricks and trips you up, blocking out the whispers from your heart in an echoing of voices that muffle the true messages that speak to your being. Let go of the constraints that man has placed upon himself over the generations, and de-emphasize the importance that has been placed upon mental intelligence. The brain is simply a tool; the heart is your source—your source of wisdom, love, Light and Universal energy. You must unblock this energy and radiate with the Light of God through your heart connection. With focus and clarity, in will come the messages that will lift you, your life and mankind into a higher level of being—where the mind and heart are open and the soul is free.

Fill the void in your life and feel the love in your heart encompassing all of humanity and life itself, for there is nothing else but love. All else pales in comparison and is created out of lack—a lack spawning the need to fill that void which can only be healed and nurtured through the Light of God. You all search and quest on a journey of self-discovery, and all journeys lead to the fulfillment of joy and love and abundance. All true joy comes from love of oneself. True love of oneself comes through love of your brothers, love of mankind, love of nature, and love of God. The

> *"The more love is shared, the more it expands and the more it fills the heart and those empty voids that leave you in relentless search and strife."*

more love is shared, the more it expands and the more it fills the heart and those empty voids that leave you in relentless search and strife.

Discover your self through your heart which holds the key to all the answers of your quest—launching you on a quickened, more direct path to self-discovery and growth. Allow this wisdom to enter directly through your heart, shutting out the naggings of your mind. One must focus bringing in this Light, as this gift is offered to all—you must simply ask and you shall receive. God's desire is that all live through their hearts lifting mankind as a whole into the enlightenment of His energy. Center there and consciously make choices and decisions based upon the wisdom that lies there within. Nothing can be forsaken, and no decision or deed can be considered unjust when one lives through the heart. Intention is key and selfless-giving is goal.

> *"The journey will travel more swiftly and gently as it will be guided through the all-seeing, all-knowing insight and wisdom of God and not by the second-guessing, nagging, questioning mind."*

When you live through the heart, you are guided by the heavens above. You may still journey a path that winds and twists with trials and tribulations, but that path will be unburdened of guilt when you center in love. The journey will travel more swiftly and gently as it will be guided through the all-seeing, all-knowing insight and wisdom of God and not by the second-guessing, nagging, questioning mind. You will also tune in to your brothers and nature, able to live in the present and truly experience that which is intended without getting trapped and lost in the fog of your mind. Let go and journey through your heart and discover what life is meant to be—a life guided through the wisdom and Light and energy of God through heartfelt feeling and focus.

> *"You are meant to shine with the Light of God and beat with the wisdom of His heart."*

You will grow as a spiritual being, resonating with the Universe in a frequency that tunes in to the pains of your brothers and the beauty of nature. You will have the wisdom to make a difference in the lives of those around and will launch your own life onto its destined path. Do not hold back your own growth and prosperity by blocking the true wisdom that is simply a heartbeat away. Quiet your mind and shut out the time-trapped limits of human thinking, and open to the greater expanse of all-encompassing wisdom that rests within your heart. You are meant to shine with the Light of God and beat with the wisdom of His heart. You are meant to share the love that is offered through God and nurture the souls of mankind, healing the wounds that are rooted in the past.

All can be dissolved and all is made clear through the wisdom that rests within and resonates through the core of your being. Take in this energy of God—focus through your mind's eye and bring it in through your heart. Listen to this wisdom and tune in to the connected hearts of your brothers. All must beat in the same rhythm, and all must dance to the same tune in order to resonate with the true power and glory of the Universe. You are all One and must all live in love to bring glory to the world and yourselves. Tune in through your heart as that is where the wisdom of God lives and breathes—creating and expanding, beating and resounding. Do your part and shine forth in love and Light, transforming your life for the love of God, your brothers and life itself.

> *"The heart is the key—*
> *the key to all and the key to the survival of mankind."*

October 11, 2009 (49 minutes)

Living Through the Heart

I am here to speak to you of what you need to know and offer to the world through heartfelt communication. When you lose your self in the recesses of your mind, you bury a part of your being—that greater part from which true wisdom resides—your heart. "Take heart" and take control of your mind to unblock the true knowing and Light within. A new day will soon dawn when the wisdom that resides in your heart will be known to all and will shine gloriously forth, unlocking the key to enlightenment and revealing the answers and vast wisdom of the Universal knowing of God.

You are all One, shining in glory beneath the buried burdens of your minds, seeking to be revealed through your hearts in order to unleash the power that is locked within. Take control of yourself and lift the Light to utilize this godly gift-of-the-heart, for this is where all wisdom resides—wisdom of your self, of your true being's purpose and of your magical, mystical, God-given gifts.

> *"You are all One, shining in glory*
> *beneath the buried burdens of your minds,*
> *seeking to be revealed through your hearts in order to*
> *unleash the power that is locked within."*

Through heartfelt communication you can touch and link to the Light of the souls that enter into your life and cross the path that you are destined to travel. Through this wisdom of the heart are truths that spring forth shedding Light upon past pains and woes. Walk hand-in-hand with your brothers toward this discovery—unraveling the mysteries and dissolving the barriers of miscommunication and misconception. All is done through understanding received through the heart, and all wisdom dwells there waiting to be unleashed and seeking to nurture and mend the wounds of your self and humanity.

> *"...in offering your heart and heartfelt wisdom to those in need, you help to heal—igniting a chain of giving or simply enabling a reprieve to a tormented soul."*

Through communication and the healing of those that you travel with or those that you meet along the journey, you nurture your own needs and soothe your own soul—reaching and accomplishing even more than you may have aspired to. With this unexpected gift of Light you enable the lifting of your own spirit, helping to lift the mass consciousness and soul of mankind, for in offering your heart and heartfelt wisdom to those in need, you help to heal—igniting a chain of giving or simply enabling a reprieve to a tormented soul.

No act of giving is in vain. No act of love is forgotten. No act of kindness goes unnoticed. And no act of selflessness is unbeneficial. You are all here to nurture and heal, to prosper and to grow. Lift your growth and your spirit-of-being to optimal heights through the nurturing of hearts

> *"No act of giving is in vain. No act of love is forgotten. No act of kindness goes unnoticed. And no act of selflessness is unbeneficial."*

and soothing of souls of those in need and those in want. Walk your path through conscious choice and heart warmth. Do not close yourself to those around you, but live to love and to learn and to connect with your fellow brethren and God, for all must live as One, connected through the Light of love that is powered and linked through the heart.

> *"The heart communicates the true essence of a situation instructing and guiding when you are tuned-in to listen. If there is a disquieting in your being that nags discontent, this signifies that the heart message is not being followed."*

The mind has its place—its place lies not in overruling judgment, but rather to aide in manifestation and in analysis of individual circumstances. The mind is a powerful tool that enables you to create from the true direction and guidance solidified through the heart. The heart communicates the true essence of a situation instructing and guiding when you are tuned-in to listen. If there is a disquieting in your being that nags discontent, this signifies that the heart message is not being followed. Tap in and tune in to what the heart is communicating, and block out the null and void stamping and stifling that emanates from the mind.

Through conditioning, mankind has been taught to discredit the heart and overemphasize the mind—to the erroneous degree that the mind is considered to be the ruler of all. That is not what was intended and has

> *"Through conditioning, mankind has been taught to discredit the heart and overemphasize the mind... That is not what was intended and has caused turmoil to mankind...delaying and blocking the progress that is meant to take place in order to achieve enlightenment."*

caused turmoil to mankind in a multitude of manifestations—delaying and blocking the progress that is meant to take place in order to achieve enlightenment.

Lift the burdens of the mind and learn to feel with your heart. The body signals when there is a conflict of the heart and mind. This is evident through illness in a battle of balance between the two forces. You must learn to reverse the process and recondition this backward thinking to live, once again, through the heart and allow it to reign as God intended, for through God-directed love only good can come and only true guidance and wisdom can spring forth.

"...the heart is the center for compassion and understanding, guidance and nurturing, love and giving. Without these, society would be mechanical and cold, unfeeling and dark."

"...there cannot be a paradise without the glory of life as seen and created through the miraculous unfolding of the heart."

That is not to say that the mind should not be utilized. Oh, on the contrary, the brain is a God-given tool engineered to record and to analyze, to weigh and to manipulate into manifestation the makings of a brilliant world. Yet it should not overtake the ruler when it not capable of such a feat, for the heart is the center for compassion and understanding, guidance and nurturing, love and giving. Without these, society would be mechanical and cold, unfeeling and dark. Love unfolds through the heart and connects you all to your Source and to each other. Stay connected and stay in-tune in order to shine forth in the love of God and the love of life—cementing your survival as a race. The mind is a miracle but must be directed from the heart in order to realize man's true potential, as there cannot be a paradise without the glory of life as seen and created through the miraculous unfolding of the heart.

Feel with your heart and open up your world and the world of those around you by giving and sharing of yourself through this godly power source. Only through true connection can you form the bonds that will bind you to your brothers and lift you into the Light of God. Awaken that glow within by opening your heart to feel what is being directed with all-knowing wisdom and guidance from Above. Take in that wisdom and cherish this gift, trusting in the all-encompassing love and nurturing that it provides.

"You will not lose your own power by sharing of yourself, but you will lift that power to a new level of understanding that can only be achieved through selfless giving and nurturing of those in need."

You will not lose your own power by sharing of yourself, but you will lift that power to a new level of understanding that can only be achieved through selfless giving and nurturing of those in need. Nothing is forgotten or abandoned when love is allowed to flow. Energy is created and directed forth, opening channels that spread and span, launching new paths of interwoven, connecting Light that link you all in a web of enlightenment. Help to thread your lives together doing your part to lift mankind and blanket the Earth in love and Light. The heart is the key— the key to all and the key to the survival of mankind.

Do not numb your life and your feeling for those that live on Earth. Do not turn your heart to stone in order to protect yourself and lock out pain. Without pain there is no growth, and there must be growth in order to reach new heights. The heart, through love, will heal and dispel all

---

"The heart, through love, will heal and dispel all pain and will connect you to each other and to your source of God."

Living Through the Heart

pain and will connect you to each other and to your source of God. This vehicle must be utilized in order to launch your life to all that it can be, all that can be experienced. You must experience life through your heart in order to truly see the beauty and gifts that the world has to offer and the wisdom that flourishes forth.

Walk with each other and cherish each other through your hearts. To do anything else would be to do a disservice to life itself and to God.

"You must experience life through your heart in order to truly see the beauty and gifts that the world has to offer and the wisdom that flourishes forth."

> *"In gratitude...you give rise to hope in a thankful prayer,*
> *lifting your spirits through means of joy*
> *and appreciation for what you have been granted."*

 *November 30, 2009 (30 minutes)*

Gratitude

I will now speak to you of gratitude and the lightness of being. In gratitude you create love for life and joy for being. You lift your spirits and your self into the Light of God, creating your world out of thanks and appreciation. You lift your life in that moment, to a higher level—manifesting forth and creating out of thin air. You give rise to hope in a thankful prayer, lifting your spirits through means of joy and appreciation for what you have been granted. You see in that moment, all that is positive—shunning away the negative, as your focus lies in abundance rather than lack. This brings about creation and change for the betterment, keeping at bay negative energies that gnaw and claw at your contentment and whittle away at your being.

Release the traps of the mind by living in gratitude, appreciating all that you have—every moment of your life. There is always a positive spin that you can put on your life, just as there is always a negative view that can take its place. It is your choice, and yours alone, with regard to how

> *"By consciously choosing to look at the positive,*
> *you turn your back and walk away from the negative,*
> *setting forth on a more fruitful, joyful, abundant path."*

you view each moment, what you choose to see, and how you examine your life. By consciously choosing to look at the positive, you turn your back and walk away from the negative, setting forth on a more fruitful, joyful, abundant path. By choosing to view things in the negative, you turn onto a dark and dreary path, destined for pain and destruction. It is always your choice as you create your own life and bring that life into fruition.

"There is always a brighter side—to everything— even if that brighter side is simply that you will never have to walk that path again..."

Let go of the constraints that twist and pull at your life, creating hardship and pain, simply by seeing the brighter side—no matter what life presents you. There is always a brighter side—to everything—even if that brighter side is simply that you will never have to walk that path again... or that you will come off that path with a bit more knowledge that you have grown into.

Walk with joy and gratitude for being, and your life will manifest into one that shines with Light and purpose. It will spring forth with vitality and creation, launching you onto your destined journey at a quicker pace—bringing you into the life that you are truly meant to live. Walk the path of negativity, and your path will wind and twist into the dark, leading you onto a journey of lost causes and struggles that present stumbling blocks that trip you up—delaying your joy in life and blocking you from your destined self-discovery.

"Walk with joy and gratitude for being, and your life... will spring forth with vitality and creation, launching you onto your destined journey at a quicker pace..."

> *"You have freewill and choice in every moment of your life."*

You have freewill and choice in every moment of your life. It may not always seem as if the choice is yours, but you always have the opportunity to determine how you view your moments—with optimism or pessimism. There is positive to everything, just as there is negative to everything. That is the balance of life. You must weigh your options and tip the scale in your own favor, or in the favor of failure and pain, suffering and loss.

It is much easier to live a life that shines in the Light of God through appreciation and gratitude, than to struggle and climb out of a rut that is steep with negativity. Once you are trapped down in that hole of distress, it is difficult to see the Light of day and claw your way back out. You will avoid much suffering if you stay focused on the positive and keep your mind from trapping you in the dark recesses of despair.

Make a conscious choice and lift your spirits, minding your thoughts through focus on the positive and good that is present in your life. There is ALWAYS something good that you can focus upon. When you focus on that good, your thoughts will continue to gravitate toward the good, lifting your life and manifesting more good to come. The opposite will happen through focus upon the negative.

Let joy surge through your moments, springing forth miracles through appreciation and gratitude—transforming your life into all that it is meant to be. That is God and that is gratitude for being.

> *"It is much easier to live a life that shines in the Light of God through appreciation and gratitude, than to struggle and climb out of a rut that is steep with negativity."*

"Humans create time, as all creatures do. It is created and expanded through 'presence in the moment'. Time is lost and abandoned through the loss of one's self to the mind's trickery."

 November 22, 2009 (53 minutes)

Capturing Time

Let us delve into the mystery of time, yet limit this information to the pursuit of enjoyment and time-fulfillment rather than to decipher the workings of time. It is much simpler to do so, and to understand. Time is a mystery locked within itself. It unravels as man lifts the burdens of his mind and settles into his heart and the feelings that reside within. The heart holds the key to this mystery and unlocks the expanse and vision-of-knowing that settles deep within the spirit-of-being.

Time whispers like the wind, traveling through a tunnel hollowed within the vision of your mind. It travels at the speed of light and then, in an instant, seems to stand still. It passes as the days go by, yet dwells—lost within the recesses of your mind—awaiting to be rediscovered through the memories of your mind. Let go of your constraints, and time travels on its own accord, seeming to have a mind of its own and an agenda written to its own desires. Time is like a broken record, etched and worn with the dust of the past, repeating itself as though it needs to be heard and revisited. Yet it can be wiped clean or tossed away, never again to be remembered.

Time is a mystery that defies the human mind. It is spun from Universal energy, created as though it were a black hole or vortex to pull and lose its resources into. It twirls and traps, encompasses and expands,

> *"It is up to the individual to experience his own reality and, therefore, to create his own time through conscious effort and conscious living."*

defies and mystifies, mortifies and delights. It is lost forever, yet remains indefinitely, unraveled and revisited through your hearts and minds, pictures and writings—recorded for eternity, yet never TRULY lived and experienced but once. It can be shaped and expanded, molded and jelled, created and lifted, lost and abandoned.

Humans create time, as all creatures do. It is created and expanded through "presence in the moment". Time is lost and abandoned through the loss of one's self to the mind's trickery. This is all a whirl of confusion to the human brain and is a mystery that can be deciphered and illustrated—yet that would encompass many chapters and volumes of text. What is of key importance and significance in regard to time, is that it is within the control of the human experience. It is up to the individual to experience his own reality and, therefore, to create his own time through conscious effort and conscious living. Time is created and expanded through the letting go of preconceived notions for what time is. It is not linear but is ever-present, reflecting forward and backward in a continuum of creation.

With each moment that you create—each moment that you consciously or fully live in the present—you are expanding your life, your time, your self and your moments of discovery. With each moment that you lose—

> *"With each moment that you create—each moment that you consciously or fully live in the present— you are expanding your life, your time, your self and your moments of discovery."*

Capturing Time

each moment that you are not present or are lost within the recesses of your mind—you are abandoning and destroying time, losing it forever for yourself or for your individual life in your present state of human existence. For those particular moments, you can never regain or recover them, as you were never actually present experiencing them. You were actually lost inside yourself—inside some daydream or thought within your head.

For those moments that you actually experience by being in a state of present consciousness, time stands still and that moment becomes deeply anchored within your soul and conscious self. Those moments live forever and are ever present, able to be recalled and relived in an instant. They live as deeply tomorrow as they do today, and as they did yesterday. They reflect and refract your life, shape and reshape it, modify and intensify it, mold and alter it. Those moments are available at your beck and call and are a part of you—a part of your heritage—a piece to pass on and a piece to build upon. They live and breathe as strongly and clearly as they did on the day that you actually experienced them.

You must cherish your moments and live them freely and thoroughly. When you do, you create ever-lasting moments of time and you expand your world to encompass on-going creation. When you are lost in the recesses of you mind, you lose your moments—your time, forever. Experience life to the fullest, taking time to enjoy it and notice its beauty and gifts. This will expand your time and the richness of your life, creating the desire to continue that expansion and, thus, continue the ever-presence in the moment, which continues to expand the existence of time, and so on. Therefore, you MUST make time for yourself, in order to make time at all.

"Enjoy your time and your life, taking time out for yourself, and you will expand and increase your time— enabling you to complete all of your responsibilities and chores, while also enjoying your life..."

There is a vast misconception that enjoyment should be set aside until the chores are finished—until the jobs are complete. If this is done, time will not be experienced for the pure sake of joy and, therefore, time will simply be whittled away—never to be experienced fully and never to be created as it should be. Enjoy your time and your life, taking time out for yourself, and you will expand and increase your time—enabling you to complete all of your responsibilities and chores, while also enjoying your life as you are meant to.

"Fully residing in the awe of God's natural beauty releases the worldly pressures of life and creates moments of true being—true living."

Experiencing nature and the enjoyment of its beauty stops time, creating ever-presence in the moment. Fully residing in the awe of God's natural beauty releases the worldly pressures of life and creates moments of true being—true living. Encompass life and all that it has to offer and your journey will unfold into a timeline of glorious moments strung together through heart-cherished beauty and wonder. You will create a glorious life, awakened to bright dawning days and love-filled memories.

Close off to life's beauty, and your memories will be clouded with lost moments of time-trapped pain and regrets for what could have been. When you live consciously and are truly in the moment, life becomes miraculous as you are present and able to see the good in the world and the love that abounds. But you must be present in order to see the glory and rise to the occasion.

"Close off to life's beauty, and your memories will be clouded with lost moments of time-trapped pain and regrets for what could have been."

Capturing Time

> *"Cherish yourself and your time. Do not waste it through needless mind-chatter, or by dwelling upon 'shoulds' or 'could have beens' or upon the negative opinions of others."*

Time can spin out of control, getting sucked into the black hole of the Universe, or it can be expanded to fill your life with wonder and glory that grows upon itself—feeding your heart with love and Light of being. It is your choice and your responsibility to grab hold of your moments and keep them from flying away—preventing them from becoming lost forever, never to be found or regained. Lock onto your time and your life simply by creating and experiencing joy, and by noticing each and every moment through glorious conscious living. Cherish yourself and your time. Do not waste it through needless mind-chatter, or by dwelling upon "shoulds" or "could have beens" or upon the negative opinions of others.

Be kind to yourself and allow yourself to be and to experience. You will be glad you did so, as you will create the "time of your life" once you actually find yourself and grant yourself the time that you deserve to gift to your life. You deserve this, and it is a must in order to enable yourself to shine forth to the world with who you actually are—and who you came to Earth to be.

> *"Life is a journey that takes time to unravel, time to create, time to nurture, time to heal, and time to offer in order to fully come to be."*

> *"As soon as you begin to fully live in the present, you will experience the expansion of time & the embracement of the fullness of your life & the unraveling of its hidden purpose."*

Life is a journey that takes time to unravel, time to create, time to nurture, time to heal, and time to offer in order to fully come to be. Step forward onto your life's path with vigor and direction, and take control over your own life by grabbing hold of your time and releasing the constraints that you have placed upon your life. As soon as you begin to fully live in the present, you will experience the expansion of time and the embracement of the fullness of your life and the unraveling of its hidden purpose.

All is encompassed within a glorious whirlwind of discovery, entrapped within the mysteries of the Universe. Time is one of the great mysteries that lies waiting to be discovered. The key to that discovery resides within your heart—where all answers lie. Live through your heart and not your mind and the mystery of time will quickly be unraveled—lifting your life and releasing your time-trapped self-imposed concerns.

"Time...is not linear but is ever-present, reflecting forward and backward in a continuum of creation."

> *"Every moment of life alters your path, your destiny, your opportunity for manifestation. To be present...gives you conscious control over your own outcome, your own path."*

 *October 18, 2009 (44 minutes)*

Conscious Living

You have a choice, a decision to make each and every moment of your life. You may look to the present moment and live in gratitude and acceptance for that moment and all that it offers and provides—all that it creates and manifests in the here and now...or you can treat that moment as a means to an end—a small moment that simply takes you to the next larger moment or course in your life. It is your choice, but do realize that there is an outcome that arises through each choice that you make in each fleeting moment of time.

 Consider the situation in which a man is walking along a path in the dark. He stumbles and falls over a branch sprouting from the Earth's surface. He has a choice in that moment, that instant, in which he must choose whether or not to reach out and cushion his fall. He has a split-second decision to make and he becomes fully conscious in that very instant, as his fate is determined by the power of his will—the choice that he makes. He reaches out and consciously decides to avoid harm coming to his physical body. He springs alive in that instant and he alters his future, avoiding the pain that would befall had he been lost in thought or trapped in the recesses of his mind. He has completely come to his senses, experiencing life to the fullest in order to arrive at a clear decisive alteration of his path. On the

other hand, had he simply fallen into the dust of the earth, he would have been scraped and bruised, harming his ego as well as his physical body. His course of action or non-action alters his path, his outcome.

Every moment of life alters your path, your destiny, your opportunity for manifestation. To be present in every moment gives you conscious control over your own outcome, your own path. It alters which direction you decide to go, which bumps you decide to step over and which branches you allow to trip you up. Your journey will go more smoothly, and you will remain more in control if your eyes stay open and focused upon the path at-hand and not on some other moment or place in time—lost in the fog of your head.

"Watch and learn, look and listen to observe the realities of your life. The filters of your mind pull veils over your vision, hindering your progress when your thoughts wander off your soul's path."

Watch and learn, look and listen to observe the realities of your life. The filters of your mind pull veils over your vision, hindering your progress when your thoughts wander off your soul's path. Stay present and allow your complete senses to properly filter in and out the criteria that is crucial to every decision that you make. Observe the beauty and wonder in the world around you. This will lift your spirits and help you to stay present

---

"Hinder not your own progress by leaving yourself in the dust of your past travels or losing yourself in the haze of your future journeys. Stay focused and in the spotlight of your current path."

in that moment of time. It will alter the outcome of your day's path which will, in turn, lead you onto a brighter more cheerful path of tomorrow.

Hinder not your own progress by leaving yourself in the dust of your past travels or losing yourself in the haze of your future journeys. Stay focused and in the spotlight of your current path. Let the sunlight filter through the trees, shedding Light upon your journey. Allow this Light to dapple and dance your life into focus with clarity and brightness. Feel the breeze and let the wings of change spread into your life. You can journey to new heights and fly forth in new flights when you focus and learn—seeing all that there is to observe and aspire to. Allow yourself to unfold and live in each and every moment with clarity and focus as you continually stay present and master your mind and your life.

"Feel as you set forth—this is a major sense that has been all but abandoned by mankind. The mind has been considered the ruler of all. Yet the mind is the culprit from which your moments flee from your grasp, causing you to lose your self in the process."

Feel as you set forth—this is a major sense that has been all but abandoned by mankind. The mind has been considered the ruler of all. Yet the mind is the culprit from which your moments flee from your grasp, causing you to lose your self in the process. Feel. Feel. Feel. Feel the present moment. Your life will blossom and the time will stand still. You will experience life as it should be and as it was meant to be—through the eyes of God and the glory of the Universe.

"You are the creator of your life, and you define your self through each moment of your experience on Earth."

Let go of the time-traps and time-warps of the mind. That is what trips you up, halting your progress and hindering your growth. Set forth on your path as if you were on a glorious vacation, relishing the moments as if they would be lost forever if not experienced with full gratitude. You are meant to journey and create your life, springing forth with vigor and definition. Define your life and define your soul, adding substance and sparkle as you take in life and God's beauty in each embraced moment. You are the creator of your life, and you define your self through each moment of your experience on Earth. Live those moments consciously—shaping your destiny and molding your self. Unblock your mind and set your spirit free in order to experience and create an incredible life of joy, luster and love.

"God grants you the moments, but you create the experience through the choices and observations that you make."

"All you have is 'now'—continuous moments of 'now'. Live in the moment as it occurs, not in the memories of your mind or in the wishes of your dreams."

God grants you the moments, but you create the experience through the choices and observations that you make. Make sound choices and guided decisions through your presence within yourself and your gifted moments of time. All you have is "now"—continuous moments of "now". Live in the moment as it occurs, not in the memories of your mind or in the wishes of your dreams. Life is meant to be experienced, and through these experiences you create your life—shaping and molding the future to come for not only yourself but for future generations and the world.

There is beauty, opportunity and growth in each moment. Do not miss what is yours for the taking, yours for the experiencing. That is a waste and a shame—for once the moment has passed, the opportunity is over and a new moment of glory and creation has already begun. Grab hold of these moments, for they are yours. Do what you will with them and allow your life to be lifted into a stream of sparkling creation that flows with energy and renewal. Do not let your mind wash away and erode your life and your spirit. Take hold of your destiny and steer your course, enjoying the ride and experiencing the waves—the ups and the downs, the rapids and the calms. All can be enjoyed by simply staying focused and clear-headed, listening to your inner guidance and relishing the beauty that is offered in each and every moment of time.

---

*"All can be enjoyed
by simply staying focused and clear-headed,
listening to your inner guidance and relishing the beauty
that is offered in each and every moment of time."*

"Enjoy where you are, when you are there. Have no regrets, as regrets are lost opportunities that can never be found."

May 27, 2009 (27 minutes)

The Flow of Life

Focus on your journey and stay present in the moment, for the moments are fleeting and are lost in an instant. Enjoy where you are, when you are there. Have no regrets, as regrets are lost opportunities that can never be found. The past is the past and is not to be focused upon but is simply what carries you to this place, floating you into this current space and time.

"Go with the current and stop fighting the rapids."

Allow yourself to be, to feel, and to go with the flow—the flow of life. Go with the current and stop fighting the rapids. There are ups and downs, but they all lead ashore where there is rest and sunlight and sandy beaches—a paradise that simply has to be found and landed upon. Struggle is what carries you there. Simply stay afloat and your destination will be found. Enjoy the wild ride, for what else is there to do? Fighting it will only prolong the journey, prolonging the struggle. What is the point of that?

"Surrender to the situation—the circumstance that shapes your learning and transforms your soul. Stop fighting the inevitable. Release, let go and let God!"

The Flow of Life 

Surrender to the situation—the circumstance that shapes your learning and transforms your soul. Stop fighting the inevitable. Release, let go and let God! It is not hopeless—it is wondrous! You will become empowered and will have the buoyancy to be lifted and carried to where you need to go—to your destined discovery—by the grace of God, the Master of Creation and the Seer of All.

Allow things to be. You then can do as you must do, enabling results to transpire, manifesting and creating beyond your visible expectation, as God envisions all—all facets, workings and effects of events and circumstances in the here-and-now and after.

 Trust and you will survive, and you may actually enjoy the ride—the ride of a lifetime, your lifetime. Let the water wash over your skin. Soak up the Sun and feel the spray and salt air. Keep you chin up. Hold your head high and do not gulp in the water in a panic of emotion, for the water can drown you with sorrows—with the pressures of life.

Believe in your skills and they will sustain you—the power is within. Call upon your resources and float high upon the crests of the waves. Nothing will turn you under. Nothing will push you down. You are powerful and you have the everlasting help of God—the buoyancy that will lift you as high as you need to go. Simply trust and be. Float and feel. Let go until you land upon the shore...and then bask in the sunlight.

"You are powerful and you have the everlasting help of God—the buoyancy that will lift you as high as you need to go. Simply trust and be."

♡

"Your current path is the only one with which to be concerned—no one else's path is of any significance to you, nor is an old worn-out path, nor a never-to-be-traveled path."

July 13, 2009 (56 minutes)

Staying On Course

Y ou all journey for a lifetime, seeking fulfillment in a time-trapped world. You must release yourself from all that holds you back and limits your flight and your growth. Once these bounds are released, the journey becomes easier and your soul flies free.

At those times when you feel frustrated and stuck, you are not living in the present moment of time but are lost elsewhere in the recesses of your mind—dwelling on a "should" or a "could have been". You are lost to a cause that has no concern with the present issue of fun and adventure, but is rather an instrument playing at your soul's torment.

Release all that drags you down and lift your eyes only to the sky that shines above. View the clouds that sparkle with the sunshine and heavenly spirit which pulls and tugs at your heartstrings, for God's gift lies within the present moment of time and space and does not dwell elsewhere. Keep your eyes focused and your vision clear, and you will see your way

"...God's gift lies within the present moment of time and space and does not dwell elsewhere. Keep your eyes focused and your vision clear..."

Staying On Course

into the bright sunshine and rainbow-Light of the Universe—the prism of color that focuses and sharpens your dreams into reality. Soar over the rainbow and find your pot of gold. Clear the fog out of your head and make way for the Light to travel into your life, for the path of least resistance is the key to all dreams come true.

 Wisdom awaits when you put one foot forward, one baby-step at a time—not looking back and not getting too far ahead of yourself. Do not stumble over your own clumsy feet, but stay focused on where you need to be, which is always in the present. Watch where you are going and not where you have been. Do not look forward or back, to the left or to the right. Your current path is the only one with which to be concerned—no one else's path is of any significance to you, nor is an old worn-out path, nor a never-to-be-traveled path.

The answers lie only in the path at hand. If you lose your focus, you will be blind-sided with doubt and despair—a journey that is not necessary and one that is a detriment to your well-being and peace of mind. Look for the answers within your soul, and rediscover how to live in the moment cherishing the gifts from God above.

Watch and learn. Look and listen. But look with your soul not your eyes. Listen with your heart not your ears, for the answers lie deeper—deeper within the spirit of mankind and God. It is where these mingle and

---

"Watch and learn. Look and listen. But look with your soul not your eyes. Listen with your heart not your ears, for the answers lie deeper..."

"You are not to jump over to another path, for your path is yours alone, and you must trust that it is sacred and special."

where they dance that the answers will form and spell out the journey that is meant to be traveled. Each individual has a path and each path has a destination. You are not to jump over to another path, for your path is yours alone, and you must trust that it is sacred and special. When you are awakened to your own resources, you will achieve all that your have set out to do—all that God has intended, and all that He has planned and put into action.

"Your steps may falter or they may be strong and sure. That is a choice that you make by staying focused and using the resources and strengths that God has bestowed upon you."

Your journey has a destination point and an arrival date. You may arrive early or you may arrive late. It depends upon how easily you can stay on course and how quickly you can rid yourself of the distractions that creep into your mind—bending the road and breaking the branches that fall onto your path trying to trip you up and force you off course.

Steer clear of these road blocks and mind bends, for they are meant to test the ground that you walk upon and shake the Earth that grounds your feet. Your steps may falter or they may be strong and sure. That is a choice that you make by staying focused and using the resources and strengths that God has bestowed upon you.

"Your journey is yours for the choosing and yours for the traveling. It is up to you to set the pace and to choose with whom you travel."

Staying On Course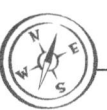

> *"...the journey begins the moment*
> *you decide to let go of the past and launch ahead."*

 Your journey is yours for the choosing and yours for the traveling. It is up to you to set the pace and to choose with whom you travel. Gather those around you or cast them to the wayside; it is your choice. Choose when to pull over to rest, but do rest your mind—for the mind can make you weary and can weaken your vision. Shake the dust from your feet and stomp off the mud. Lighten the load by lightening your mind and you will travel with less baggage to weigh you down and make you tired, lifting the desire to sit in stagnation—for the journey begins the moment you decide to let go of the past and launch ahead.

Your steps will slow and falter when your mind is cluttered with worry and distraction—distraction that has no place when your concentration is needed to focus upon the path that you are climbing. Climb only ahead, not around in circles which lead you back to places that you have already been—places to which you have already journeyed. Why circle the mountain over and over again...never getting ahead, only sticking in the mud, sliding and climbing back to a safe place to rest—only to struggle back to that place once more? No! Climb on out of the muck, leaving what is meant to be left behind.

Explore higher ground, lifting yourself to the next level of development, seeking a path of joy and less resistance. Watch and you will see a transformation of your own soul as you journey the path into the unforeseen.

> *"...venture forth and get unstuck from*
> *your mind's grasp upon your soul, for within your soul*
> *dwells the key and the map to discovery..."*

> *"...let go of the anxiety that brings you down and cripples your mind, blocking and stockading your confidence and freedom..."*

There is much to be explored and discovered, but you must journey forth in order to discover it. Do not let road blocks dissolve your efforts. Seek enlightenment and growth, and before your eyes transformation will occur. A beauty beyond your wildest dreams will manifest into reality, but only if you venture forth and get unstuck from your mind's grasp upon your soul, for within your soul dwells the key and the map to discovery—one that will launch you into a lifetime of achievement and dreams of grandeur. Follow your heart's wildest dreams, and let go of the anxiety that brings you down and cripples your mind, blocking and stockading your confidence and freedom—freedom from the bonds of passage.

Walk hand-in-hand with God and you will be led into the Light and onto a path of sunshine and wealth—a wealth that flows like a stream of golden opportunity that runs rich and deep, gathering and banking into a world that reflects images of man's reality merged with nature and God. God is the Source, the gulf of the unknown waters—the endless supply that feeds man's thirst and quenches his desire for prosperity and abundance. God delivers the riches of the Earth, spreading its resources and filtering the soot out of the mouths of cascading streams—streams of consciousness that can drown the self when the mind whirls with worry and anxiety or thirsts beyond control.

> *"God is the provider, the one to call upon, the one that gives buoyancy to the spirit, lifting it into the Light and back on course...to achieve its higher purpose..."*

Staying On Course

God is the provider, the one to call upon, the one that gives buoyancy to the spirit, lifting it into the Light and back on course—back in the direction that it must head in order to achieve its higher purpose and that which is intended by God Himself.

Watch and revel in the glory of the Kingdom of Paradise which is found only in the present moment. It lies in the heart of nature and should not be buried beneath the burdens and distractions of your mind, but revealed by your soul's watery spirit—a spirit spurting with life, overflowing with joy, and bursting with power. Stand tall and stand firmly in the present, refusing to look where there is no need to look. Remove yourself from the distractions in order to let life's river of wealth and opportunity flow abundantly free—washing away the pains and struggle and carrying forth peace and love, prosperity and joy.

To live in Light and glory is to shine in the Light of God, lifting your soul and the souls of mankind onto the path of enlightenment.

"Remove yourself from the distractions in order to let life's river of wealth and opportunity flow abundantly free—washing away the pains and struggle and carrying forth peace and love, prosperity and joy."

You must launch your own ship of magnificence in order to discover your journey and purpose. You must ride the waves and expand your horizons, banishing the fear and misconception that anchor and keep you from leaving the shore. Once you set sail, you will discover your seafaring ways and will launch ahead on your adventure.

There will be storms to weather in order to learn lessons and bring about change, but the hardship will cease when the seas are calmed and the ship is mastered. You cannot master your own ship if you will not take the wheel and steer its course. Without proper guidance and action the ship will crash against the rocks and sink, drowning your soul—that soul which is meant to sail those seas on an adventure of a lifetime.

The seas will be calmed when your spirit or soul is calmed—when you learn to trust and find peace, listening to the whispers of the wind, that voice of God that sings and sirens through the heart. You will then steer clear of the disasters that approach, avoiding future hardship and pain—sailing into the discovery of your destined glory.

Let go of your fears and release your worries to God, for He has the power to dispel all and has the vision to set you straight on course into discovery and growth, awakening and transformation. Set sail, launching your ship of miracles into the Light and beauty of the rising Sun!

www.ingramcontent.com/pod-product-compliance
Lightning Source LLC
Chambersburg PA
CBHW050625300426
44112CB00012B/1661